D1546170

THE SOCIAL HISTORY OF EDUCATION

GENERAL EDITOR: VICTOR E. NEUBURG

First Series — No. 6

MEMORANDUM ON POPULAR EDUCATION

THE SOCIAL HISTORY OF EDUCATION

GENERAL EDITOR: VICTOR E. NEUBURG

First Series of Eight Titles

MEMORANDUM

ON

POPULAR EDUCATION

SIR JAMES KAY SHUTTLEWORTH

AUGUSTUS M. KELLEY PUBLISHERS
New York 1969

Published by
WOBURN BOOKS LIMITED
9 RUSSELL CHAMBERS, BURY PLACE, LONDON WC1

Published in the United States by
Augustus M. Kelley, Publishers
New York, New York 10010

First edition   1868
New impression   1969

Printed in Holland by
N.V. Grafische Industrie Haarlem

MEMORANDUM

ON

POPULAR EDUCATION.

BY

SIR JAMES KAY-SHUTTLEWORTH, Bart.

LONDON:
RIDGWAY, PICCADILLY.

PRICE ONE SHILLING.

NOTICE TO THE READER.

THE author of the enclosed Memorandum has hoped that he might, without presumption, contribute towards the impending discussions on Popular Education in Parliament a faithful analysis of the present state of that question, stripped of those technicalities which have served to obscure it, and to make legislative and administrative error more practicable. If he has succeeded in accomplishing this task in a calm and judicial spirit and with due respect to the great ability and patriotic motives of those whose measures he has without reserve examined, he has also recorded the results without deference to any authority or force but that of truth.

38, *Gloucester Square, Hyde Park, W.*
January 24th, 1868.

MEMORANDUM

ON THE

PRESENT STATE OF THE QUESTION

OF

POPULAR EDUCATION.

THE attention of both Houses of Parliament has recently been called in an emphatic manner to popular education.

Her Majesty, in opening Parliament at the commencement of the session recently adjourned, said, "The general question of " the education of the people requires your most serious attention, " and I have no doubt that you will approach the subject with a " full appreciation both of its vital importance and of its acknow- " ledged difficulty." And the Chancellor of the Exchequer, re- ferring to this portion of the Queen's Speech, is thus reported :— "The passage referring to education is not a mere rhetorical " flourish. Her Majesty's Government have given their most " earnest attention to the subject, but as Parliament has been " called together in November, we should not feel justified in " referring more specifically to our efforts and intentions in that " direction."

Lord Russell, to whose foresight and perseverance this great question owes so much, after a speech in the House of Lords, in which he reviewed the whole subject, moved a comprehensive series of resolutions, giving an outline of the principles of future legislation.

The announcements of the intentions of the Government are a natural consequence of the recent great extension of electoral power among the classes supported by manual labour. The beneficial exercise of that power will be a measure of the intelli- gence and virtue of the classes who are most to be influenced by primary education. All are agreed that a well-ordered system of national education, reaching to the most ignorant and desti- tute, would be the firmest foundation on which our widely-spread electoral power could rest.

Up to this time, the Government has promoted the founda- tion and improvement of schools by the administration of public grants, but has left the initiative to the churches and congregations of religious communions. While the Committee of Council have encouraged the extension of this system, they have devoted by far the larger part of their grants to ensure the efficiency of the schools thus founded. That efficiency, as the experience of Europe and America proves, must be directly proportionate to the character, skill, and number of the teachers. The creation and employment of a body of trained teachers and assistants have therefore been regarded by the Government as indispensable conditions, without which the building of schools could have little effect.

Whatever may be the sources whence the income of the schools may be derived—how abundant soever that income may be—under whatever management each school may be placed—by whatever local or central administration the inspection and regulation of schools may be conducted—and whatever may be the course of instruction intended to be given—all must fail to exert a civilizing influence on the people, unless the teachers are in numbers, skill, and knowledge equal to the duty they have to discharge.

Various powerful motives have promoted the growth and improvement of primary education, especially since 1846. But the recent extension of the franchise superadds one which has never before operated with the same force. There is now a clear political necessity to fit the electors for the right exercise of their power.

Recent opportunities for the comparison of our own inventive, constructive, and decorative arts with those of foreign countries, have inspired a conviction that the more thorough primary instruction of such countries as Prussia, and the opportunities afforded to their artisans for that superior education which leads to a knowledge of the technical relations of science and the arts, afford to foreign workmen advantages which ours must have in order to maintain a successful competition.

The anti-social doctrines held by the leaders of Trades' Unions as to the relations of capital and labour, and their consequent organization to limit the freedom of workmen and masters by a system of terror, have been again exposed by inquiries under the Trades' Union Commission. Parliament is again warned how much the law needs the support of sound economic opinions and higher moral principles among certain classes of workmen, and how influential a general system of public education might be in rearing a loyal, intelligent, and Christian population.

Whatever has been hitherto done towards this result has been accomplished in spite of controversies so formidable, that the whole national power has never been employed, but only partial, yet great forces have been combined, and the foundation of a national system has slowly been laid.

It may therefore be useful to glance rapidly at the successive steps by which the Government has availed itself of whatever spontaneous zeal existèd, and endeavoured so to guide the voluntary associations as to render their co-operation with the State consistent with its paramount duty to secure for every child that education, without which life itself is a doubtful blessing.

The Government commenced its work timidly, and continued it feebly for several years.

The Grants of the Treasury to the National and British and Foreign School Society, from 1832 to 1839, provided simply for the extension of education by the building of schools connected with those two societies. The Government did not even interfere to secure the improvement of the character of the school buildings—an object to which they have devoted so much attention since that time.

Lord Russell's letter to Lord Lansdowne in 1839 first introduced the idea of the improvement of the methods of instruction, and the qualifications of schoolmasters. It proposed to form a Model School, to provide for inspection, and to increase the number of teachers. It also defined the basis of a system of public education in the expression of " Her Majesty's wish that " the youth of this kingdom should be religiously brought up, " and that the rights of conscience should be respected," and pointed to " the neglect of this great subject among the enact-" ments of our voluminous legislation."

From 1839 to 1846 strenuous efforts, many of which were baffled, were made to carry out these proposals. Owing to these failures, only 305,000*l.* were expended in these seven years by the Committee of Council, in promoting by grants the building of schools, on improved plans and with better internal arrangements, and in founding and extending inspection.

In the interval, successive ministries had been defeated, once in an attempt to found a Normal College—again in the provision of schools for children employed in factories—and in various subordinate efforts. Thus checked, the Government acted on the principle of stimulating and aiding the efforts of voluntary associations, but up to 1846 they had made no grants to promote the efficiency of instruction. The obstacles to this efficiency were—the want of competent teachers, and of any sufficient means for their training—the absence of any staff of skilled assistants—and of suitable books and apparatus.

The Committee of Council therefore submitted to Parliament

their Minutes of 1846. The intention of these Minutes was to give an impulse to the growth and improvement of the system founded by the religious communions, and the efficiency of which had been increased by the Government Grants and by inspection.

Henceforth the Education Department directly encouraged the introduction of a more adequate staff of more skilful teachers. It made the schools the scenes of the first five years of the teacher's training. It selected from the classes immediately in contact with the people, and generally from children of the manual-labour class, their future instructors—ensuring an identity of interest and harmonious sympathies. It confided the completion of their training to the religious communions, who founded numerous colleges in which the approved candidates spent two years. It strove to employ the energy of religious zeal, by liberal encouragement from the Parliamentary Grant, in rearing and training a body of highly instructed teachers, who throughout their experience should breathe the air of the school and be in contact with the humblest classes. The extension of popular education would thus proceed *pari passu* with its improvement. A few years would prove how far the voluntary initiative would suffice, with the aid of the Government, to reach the degraded classes of the great cities and the apathetic parishes of remote rural districts. The Department would ascertain whether any other expedient was necessary to rescue children who were doomed to ignorance by the poverty or vices of their parents in cities, or by their apathy and helplessness in farming districts.

A great impulse was thus given to the exertions of the religious bodies. The majority of them entered earnestly into this co-operation. The whole sum of the Parliamentary Grants, which had amounted in the seven years between 1839 and 1846 to only 305,000*l*., rose to an outlay of 6,405,862*l*. in the sixteen succeeding years.[*]

The Grants of the Committee of Council were at the average rate of about one-third[†] of the local outlay on building and supporting elementary schools. Bearing this in mind, a brief analysis of the distribution of the Parliamentary Grant will give some impression of the influence of the Minutes of 1846 on the extension and improvement of primary education.

The sum of the grants for building, enlarging, and furnish-

---

[*] See Minutes, 1862–63, p. 1., where the whole expenditure from 1839 to 31st December, 1862, is stated to be 6,710,862*l*. 14*s*. 10*d*. If 305,000*l*. be deducted from this, the remainder, 6,405,862*l*., represents the outlay in the period intervening between 1846 and 1862.

[†] See p. 67, Report of Royal Commission on State of Popular Education.

ing schools amounted in 1866 to 1,608,100*l.*,* and with this aid 6,801 schools, capable of accommodating 915,516 scholars, had been built.† The annual grants ‡ towards the expenses of maintaining elementary schools since 1839 had become in the aggregate 5,297,210*l.*, of which 3,714,899*l.* had been directly applied to the keeping up of an efficient staff of teachers. These aggregates represent only one-third of the actual expenditure, which exceeded twenty millions. At the last annual inspection, 1,234,491 scholars were present. The grants towards the support of training colleges—which were in the ratio of two-thirds of the annual outlay—amounted in 1866 to 1,046,443*l.*§ All notice of some small subordinate objects of expenditure is omitted. The cost of administration had been 912,647*l.*, of which the greater portion arose from the Inspection and Examination Departments, by which the efficiency of schools was so greatly promoted.

This outlay of upwards of twenty millions drew every religious communion, except the Congregational Dissenters, and bodies allied with them, into co-operation with the Government. It created a vast denominational system, which firmly established popular education on a religious basis. All efforts to promote a secular, or purely civil system, supported by rates, and governed solely by rate-payers, outside the pale of religious organization, failed. But the Government did not procure the recognition of religious rights in all these schools. The idea of a school founded for national objects, and working in harmony with civil and religious liberty, was of slow growth. Thus, much resistance was offered to the association of the lay members of congregations with the clergy in the management of schools. Still greater difficulties have prevented the legal recognition, in the Trust Deeds, of the rights of Dissenters to have their children educated in schools supported by public money without any sacrifice of religious feeling or opinion. The time had approached when it was necessary that this vast denominational system should be made to work in harmony with civil rights, and with the political wants of the State.

Several objects not recognized In the Minutes of 1846 had become the subjects of grants. A Capitation Grant, introduced by a Special Minute in 1853, and intended only to apply to purely rural parishes, had been extended to the urban districts. The individual examination of the scholars in the three rudiments, by which the distribution of this grant was to have been regulated, had not been carried out. No measures had been

---

* Minutes, 1866–67, p. civ.
‡ Ibid., 1866–67, p. civ.
† Ibid., 1866–67, p. cx.
§ Ibid., p. civ.

adopted to restrain the excess of the grants above the legitimate claims of certain classes of schools. Generally the administration had a tendency to become lavish and indiscriminating. These were faults which ought to have been corrected by the department.

Moreover, rapidly as the tide of education had advanced, the apathy of certain districts presented obstacles not to be removed by a system which depended on a voluntary initiative. In its flow, this tide also had broken upon barriers of resistance. The young and raw teachers had a task which would have baffled the wisest. They had to train a migratory, ignorant, and rude population. That civilization which can only be the result of generations of culture was expected from their hands in a few years. The acknowledged imperfections of the schools were attributed, rather to the incapacity of the teachers, than to their inadequate numbers, and to the extreme difficulties of their work. On these, and on many other accounts, it was conceived, in 1859, that the time had arrived when a Royal Commission might with advantage examine the whole operation of this system. This Commission, composed of men of great ability, representing every phase of political and religious opinion, devoted nearly three years to a faithful and exhaustive inquiry, and presented·in 1861 a Report, in which, with judicial calmness, they approve the main features of the operations of the Committee of Council, and especially those which provided for the training of a body of teachers by means of the five years' apprenticeship, and of two years' College education.

In this Report, suggestions were made in the hope of securing the civil rights of minorities :—of gradually introducing the spirit and power of local action, in aid of the central administration, and of simplifying the action of the Education Department. For this purpose, a County Board was to be appointed, and to have charge of one form of capitation grants to be derived from the county rates. It was thus intended to relieve the pressure on the central administration and the Parliamentary Grant. The distribution of this County Capitation Grant was to be determined by the results of an examination of the scholars in reading, writing, and arithmetic, to be conducted by County Examiners. These provincial grants were also intended to provide for the extension of the system into the poorest and most apathetic districts.

On the other hand, the Central inspection was to be continued, and was to have charge of the general character of the school, the entire scope of instruction, the methods, organization, and discipline, as well as of the superintendence of the training of apprentices, and of the examinations by which the progress of their education was tested. As the results of this inspection, two classes of grants might be obtained when the state of the school was satisfactory. One was adjusted to the average attendance of scholars—the other was dependent on the employment of one pupil-teacher for every 30 scholars, or of one assistant for every 60. The Central and the County Grants were not together to exceed either the fees and subscriptions, or 15s. per child in average attendance. As a whole, the recommendations of the Royal Commission confirmed with its sanction the operations of the Committee of Council, and cautiously sought to co-ordinate the voluntary religious agencies with national action, through the local, as well as the central civil power. These suggestions evinced a wise sympathy with the labours and sacrifices which had built up what then existed of the framework of a national system of education, and especially with the machinery of instructed teachers who had charge of the difficult task of training the children of a hardy, energetic, but unlettered and often sensual people. If adopted, these plans would, at least, have caused no discouragement or shock. They would rather have enriched than impoverished the schools, while they diffused the grants more equally: and under them the Managers would have had sufficient motives to keep up the efficiency and numbers of the teaching staff.

The objects sought to be attained by the Royal Commission are summed up in the following words (pp. 327–8):—" We " shall propose means by which, *in the first place*, the present " system may be made applicable to the poorer no less than the " richer districts throughout the whole country: *secondly*, by " which the present expenditure may be controlled and regu- " lated: *thirdly*, by which the complication of business in the office " may be checked : *fourthly*, by which greater local activity and " interest in education may be encouraged: *fifthly*, by which the " general attainment of a greater degree of elementary know- " ledge may be secured than is acquired at present."

To the Committee of Council, as the executive department, fell the duty of reviewing these recommendations, and of proposing to Parliament a modification of the existing system founded upon them. This gave rise, in 1862, to the Revised Code.

The provisions of the Revised Code—though introduced with great ability—had a very different tendency. All that part of the recommendations of the Royal Commission which related to the localization of the administration, and the employment of Examiners in addition to Inspectors, was omitted.

The Grants which had been given to maintain the number and efficiency of the Teachers were withdrawn. The conditions of the Capitation Grant substituted for them were such as to cut down the rate of aid (as we shall see) from 12s. 3d. per head to 8s. 6d., or to nearly half the maximum proposed by the Commissioners. The amount of this reduction has, however, exceeded the intentions of the authors of the Revised Code, who expected that the average rate would amount to 10s. per scholar.

The conditions as to the employment of Pupil Teachers were so relaxed, that a master might have 89 scholars without the aid of an apprentice or assistant teacher. The Inspectors, instead of a separate class of examiners, were charged with the individual examination of the scholars in reading, writing, and ciphering. Their attention was thus withdrawn from the higher subjects of instruction and the general condition of the school. The Capitation Grant was so apportioned according to the results of this examination as practically to discourage higher instruction. The provisions securing the training of the Pupil Teachers, and making it the interest of the teachers to give them regular instruction, were injuriously relaxed. According to the popular interpretation of this Code, the limits of elementary instruction were—so much knowledge of reading, writing, and arithmetic as could be attained before eleven years of age ;—and the best means to attain this end were the concentration of the work of the school on a drill in these three rudiments.

We may conceive that a statesman who had deliberately made this change, had conceived that the material necessities of the manual-labour class rendered hopeless any higher result of primary education, than a fair proficiency in reading, writing, and arithmetic, and that the machinery, created by the Minutes of 1846, prepared teachers too highly instructed for so useful yet humble an object. It might therefore have been the intention of the Committee of Council to make the education of the Pupil Teachers and Certificated Masters less comprehensive, and to introduce a humbler order. At the same time the Department may have hoped that a part of the burthen of the Parliamentary Grant could be shifted onto the local Managers, and that their greater exertions and sacrifices would supply from local sources what was withdrawn from central. Moreover, it might have been intended that the intelligence and zeal of the Managers should be tested by confiding to them many details which had hitherto been the subject of official regulation. If the local administration failed in these particulars, it would fall into discredit, and the way would be cleared for a change of system.

If the authors of the Revised Code expected that local intelligence and zeal would supply by increased contributions the income withdrawn by the Government from the schools, or would keep up the efficiency and numbers of the teaching-staff when the conditions of the grants were relaxed, that expectation was by no means fulfilled.

No scheme of public education is likely to obtain sanction which does not recognize and define the functions of the Education Department, and enable it by Minutes laid before Parliament to provide for the training of teachers, and the maintenance by various means of the standard of instruction. The Manchester and Salford Education Bill of 1852, Lord Russell's Boroughs Education Bill of 1853, and the measure introduced last session by Mr. Bruce, while they all provide in a similar manner for a local rate in aid of the resources of schools, likewise contemplate the continuance of the system of public grants from the Committee of Council on Education. The principles on which such grants are administered, and the details of the regulations by which they are to be carried out, are therefore, under such a system, as important as when the schools otherwise depended only on local spontaneous agencies. It is on this account important that the results of the change made by the Revised Code should be carefully analyzed, for from these results we may ascertain how far it is possible, without injurious consequences, to relax the conditions of the public grants.

One of the principal objects of the Revised Code obviously was to introduce *an economy in the administration of the Parliamentary Grant.** With a reduced rate of aid, the efficiency of the schools could still be maintained, if the voluntary contributions and school-pence supplied the proportion of public grant withdrawn. Regarded as a financial attempt to adjust, in this way, the incidence of the charge for elementary education without crippling its resources, we have to inquire whether or in what degree, the aid withdrawn by the Revised Code from elementary schools has been replaced from local and voluntary sources.

The expenditure of the Committee of Council reached its maximum in the year ending December 31st, 1861, when it amounted to 813,441*l.* In that year 6,764 schools, under separate management, with an average attendance of 855,077 scholars,† were inspected. The grants made to these elementary day-schools amounted to 525,425*l.*,‡ or they were at the rate of 12*s.* 3*d.* per scholar.§ In the year preceding December 31st,

---

* Mr. Lowe, in introducing the Revised Code on the 13th February, 1862, is reported to have said, " I cannot promise the House that this system will be an " economical one ; and I cannot promise that it will be an efficient one : but I can " promise that it shall be either the one or the other. If it is not cheap, it shall be " efficient ; if it is not efficient, it shall be cheap."—*Hansard*, p. 229, vol. clxv.

† See Minutes, 1861, p. 3 and p. 7.   ‡ Ibid., 1861–2, p. xlvii.

§ See Minutes, 1859–60, where it is stated to be 11*s.* 6*d.* per scholar in England and Wales. Also Report of Commissioners on Popular Education, p. 67.

1866, the whole expenditure had been reduced to 622,730*l*. But though the outlay was less by 190,711*l*. in 1866 than in 1861, 1,539 more schools in receipt of annual grants had been inspected, and there was an average attendance of 141,633 more scholars. The grants made directly to elementary day-schools in 1866* amounted to 445,714*l*. for an average attendance of 1,048,493 scholars, or they were at the rate of 8*s*. 6*d*. per scholar. The rate of aid from the Government towards the support of elementary day-schools had therefore been reduced at the rate of 3*s*. 9*d*. per scholar between 1861 and 1866 ; but the income of the schools from local and voluntary sources had, in the same period, increased only at the rate of 1*s*. 1*d*. per scholar, so that the annual resources of the schools had been reduced at the rate of two shillings and eightpence (2*s*. 8*d*.) per head. The reduction of three shillings and ninepence in the Government grant, with an average attendance of 1,048,493 scholars in 1866, represents 196,592*l*., withdrawn by the Committee of Council from what would have been the annual income of the day-schools, if the rate of aid per scholar had continued to be as high as in 1861. Of this loss, one shilling and one penny per scholar was returned by voluntary local agencies, leaving the annual resources of the schools diminished by 139,799*l*., which these voluntary agencies had been unable to supply. The whole increase from local resources did not amount to one-third the loss from the public grants.

The sources from which the increase of 1*s*. 1*d*. per scholar was derived, are apparent from an inspection of Table No. 1.

The school-pence increased from about 7*s*. 7*d*. per scholar in 1861 to 8*s*. 6*d*. in 1866, or about elevenpence per head ; and the local income from endowments, voluntary subscriptions, and other sources, from about 9*s*. 9¾*d*. per scholar, in 1861, to 10*s*. 0¼*d*., in 1866, or about twopence halfpenny per head. If the reduction of the annual grants effected by the Revised Code was made with the intention of stimulating local exertions, and the expectation that the amount of public aid withdrawn would be replaced by private contributions, the failure was complete, for such increased contributions amounted only to one-eighteenth part of the amount of grants withdrawn. From school-pence, however, one-fourth was derived. Nevertheless, the resources of the schools were crippled, and before analyzing the effects of the Code on the machinery of schools, it may be well to examine the direct influence of the reduction of income, and of the conditions of the Capitation Grant, on the instruction of the scholars.

---

* Minutes, 1866–7, p. civ.

The expedient of making the aid of the Committee of Council *mainly* depend on Capitation Grants, the amount of which is to be determined by the individual examination of the scholars, is open to some fundamental objections.

The deductions on examination for failures in reading, writing, and arithmetic are by no means a sufficient test of the efficiency or teaching power of a school. The number of scholars who pass in the Standards of the Revised Code is relatively less in a migratory population—like that of the poorest parts of cities, and the outskirts of the manufacturing districts —for in such places, the children enter the school ignorant, and stay so short a time as to be unable to acquire the rudiments. Thus a school in an apathetic district, supported only by the lowest resources from voluntary agencies, may have the hardest task, and receive the lowest rate of aid; or, a school in which the intelligence and liberality of the Managers has maintained the teaching power in the utmost efficiency as to numbers and skill, may, from the ignorance and migratory character of the population, earn a grant far below the ratio of its outlay or merit, and even below the average. Any grant, the amount of which is determined by individual examination after a certain attendance at School, tends to cause the neglect of the irregular, dull, and migratory scholars whom *it does not pay to teach;* while, on the other hand, grants proportionate to the average attendance of scholars are a direct inducement to fill the School, but not to teach the children, if such grants are not accompanied by conditions as to the number of the teaching staff.*

---

* In a letter to Lord Granville, dated April 24th, 1861, the author thus stated, in another form, some of these difficulties:—" Any Capitation Grant, the distribu-
" tion of which is to be determined by the results of instruction in schools, is
" liable to the fundamental objection, that the average period of the attendance of
" the majority of scholars is so short, that, as far as that majority is concerned,
" few schools would be paid for the results of their own work. In the specimen
" districts, 42·3 per cent. of the scholars (p. 659) had been in the same public week-
" day school less than one year, and 22·7 per cent. had been one year, but less than
" two years. These proportions for England and Wales are 41·65 per cent. of the
" scholars who had attended the same school less than one year, and 22·58 who
" had been one year, and less than two years. With such migratory scholars, it is
" impossible justly to pay for work done in schools on any plan constructed to
" embrace those three-fifths of the scholars who attend less than two years. The
" remaining 35·77 per cent. who attend more than two years are alone subjects for
" an examination of the results secured by the work in any school. This, however,
" is not the proposal of the Commission. Their proposal is to pay a Capitation
" Grant on every scholar who has attended 140 days in the preceding year, and can
" read, write, and cipher. A scholar cannot learn to read, write, and cipher, so as
" to pass a public examination in two years, much less in 140 days. Any examina-
" tion of the majority of more than three-fifths who attend less than two years
" must, therefore, obviously fail to ascertain how far even these elements have been
" taught to that majority in any school. If the remaining two-fifths who have
" been in the school more than two years were separated from the other scholars,
" and examined apart, some approximate estimate might be thus made of the work

Thus the Revised Code fails to penetrate the poorest, most ignorant, and migratory districts, which are also generally the most apathetic.* And its grants are by no means proportionate to the intelligence and zeal of the Managers.

On the other hand, schools which contrive their machinery strictly with a view to enable their scholars to pass mechanically the examination of the Revised Code in the Standards of reading, writing, and arithmetic, without cultivating their general intelligence, may earn a Capitation Grant considerably above the average, though the civilizing power of such schools is low.†

The Committee of Council thus describe another consequence of the increase of the pecuniary risks of the Managers, consequent on the substitution of the Capitation Grant, and of the reduction of the rate of aid to schools. This has, at least in some districts, become common. " In some cases, the Mana- " gers exhibit an inclination to throw the whole pecuniary risk " on the teachers, thereby reducing the schools to the level of a " private adventure ; placing themselves in a highly questionable " position as to the worth of the certificates of character which

---

" done in the school. If any Grant could be devised, founded on the results of the " school work, it must be proportioned only to the proficiency of this two-fifths of " the scholars. But the working of such a Grant was long ago examined and " rejected as full of difficulties which appeared insuperable."—*Four Periods of Public Education.* Longman, pp. 568–569.

* The Rev. John Menet, in a pamphlet, published by Rivington in 1865, remarks on the unequal distribution of a Capitation Grant between town and country schools, and on the Registers of the attendance of scholars, as follows :— " It would be easy to show, if this were the place for it, that a Capitation Grant " is essentially vicious in principle, and that the assistance given upon this basis " must always be in inverse proportion to the need, inasmuch as large town-schools " with the most regular attendance would receive far more in proportion than the " smaller country schools, or town-schools with shifting populations, while, in fact, " they need it far less. Nor is it right that large Grants of public money should " be paid by the State upon the vouchers of those interested in receiving the Grants " without the possibility of checking those vouchers. And yet this must be done in " the case of a Capitation Grant on attendance ; for the money must be paid upon " the returns of the School Registers marked by the teachers themselves."†

‡ The Rev. John Menet, in the pamphlet already quoted, thus describes the effect of the inspection on the methods and character of instruction in schools (p. 7) :—" The results which are paid for under the Revised Code, are to a great " extent, produced mechanically. Children may be taught to read correctly out of " a book in use in the school (which they may know nearly by heart), and be " taught to write a sentence from dictation correctly, out of one of the reading " books, without any development of their intelligence, and without any approach " to cultivation of mind. It would not be difficult to avoid any gross failure in " the religious knowledge. It might be less easy to secure the children from " failure in arithmetic ; but even supposing that they were less successful in this " subject, a grant would still be payable upon the reading and writing. The " fact is, that the 'results' under the Revised Code may be, and are produced " to a very great extent, by mechanical means. And the result is, that the State " is daily paying grants in aid of schools which do, or need do, scarcely anything " towards the real work of a school properly so called. It is a condition of " existence that these 'results' should be produced, because they are worth so " much money."

" are required from them ; and lastly, surrendering all power to
" direct the instruction and practice of the school in any other
" course than that which appears, however shortsightedly, to lead
" the nearest way to a grant." Nor is it possible to overlook
in such cases the dependence of a part of the Grant on the
accuracy of the register of attendance, and the absence of the control of the managers to ensure that accuracy, when the teacher's
interests are directly concerned in increasing the number of
scholars apparently attending the school. At least the Revised
Code ought not to place obvious temptations in the way of the
teacher to record the presence of every scholar, however late, or
when merely the bearer of an excuse for absence.

But passing from these general objections. The system
under the Revised Code is, as we have seen, cheaper. Is it
more or less efficient? In his very able and exhaustive statement of the principles of the Revised Code, Mr. Lowe said,*
" We deal with schools on this principle:—If they are effective
" in their teaching, they shall receive public aid to the amount
" which the commissioners have declared to be sufficient; but
" if they are not effective, they shall not receive it. In this way
" we make a double use of our money. It not only enables the
" schools to afford instruction, but it encourages them to aug-
" ment the quantity of that education. It is a spur to improve-
" ment; it is not a mere subsidy, but a motive for action; and I
" have the greatest hopes of the improved prospects of education,
" if this principle is embraced." *The method of examination, and
the mode of distributing the annual grants under the Revised Code,*
were intended to secure more constant attention to the instruction
of junior classes, and greater proficiency in reading, writing, and
arithmetic. For this purpose, the grants which had been previously awarded directly to the teachers for the purpose of
maintaining a sufficient staff of efficient teachers and assistants,
were commuted into Capitation Grants, given partly for a
certain number of days' attendance, and partly in proportion to
the number of scholars who might pass in each of the three
rudimentary subjects of instruction.

It may be expedient, first, to observe the effects of the
Code on the instruction in the school apart from its influence on
the machinery of education. The authors of the Code were
warned by many who had much experience in elementary
education, that the plan adopted would discourage the cultivation of any instruction higher than the rudiments,† and would
introduce a mechanical method of teaching. They also urged
that a school from which the higher subjects were excluded,

---

* Hansard, p. 230, vol. clxv.   † See Minutes, 1865–6, p. 16.

would be generally less successful in the lower. The Committee of Council now say*—" The Revised Code has tended, at " least temporarily, to discourage attention to the higher " branches of elementary instruction: Geography, Grammar, " History. There are signs of recovery, and those schools do " best in the elementary subjects where the higher are " not neglected." But the intentions of the authors of the Revised Code have not been fulfilled by the greater proficiency of the scholars in the rudiments of reading, writing, and ciphering.

The percentages of failure in the Standards in 1863-4, when compared with those of 1866, show an increase of failures in 1866, in all of the Standards above Standard I., except in reading under Standard VI., and in writing in Standards II. and VI. The following table exhibits the amount of this failure in each Standard of examination :†—

	READING.		WRITING.		ARITHMETIC.	
	1863-4.	1866.	1863-4.	1866.	1863-4.	1866.
Standard I. ..	20·2	13·73	17·68	10·61	26·77	20·15
Standard II. ..	10·85	11·73	8·05	5·26	25·25	26·63
Standard III. ..	6·4	8·24	15·35	21·10	18·95	24·11
Standard IV. ..	4·6	6·22	19·62	27·28	18·25	31·61
Standard V. ..	5·35	5·44	14·11	17·40	16·98	25·11
Standard VI. ..	5·93	4·76	12·85	12·55	16·49	23·92

* Report, Minutes, 1865-6, p. xiii.

† I have been furnished by a clergyman who has great practical knowledge of the working of the Revised Code, with the following remarks on the system of the individual examination of the scholars by standards rather than, as formerly, by classes :—" But one great and fatal bar to the real progress of education in " elementary schools under the Revised Code is the system of individual examina- " tion by standards, to determine the amount of the Capitation Grant, and for the " following among other reasons :—

" 1. A measure of attainment to be required of all schools must of necessity be " the *minimum* of attainment.

" 2. But it is equally clear that as that amount will secure the Grant, the " *minimum* becomes the *maximum*.

" 3. There arises a direct temptation, or perhaps necessity, to organize the school " by *standards* instead of *classes*. The effects are that as an advance of only one " standard per year is necessary to earn the Grant, it is the interest of the teacher " to keep the child in the standard during the whole year, though he might be, " both by ability and acquirements, entitled to be placed far above it. It is also " the teacher's interest to place every scholar in the lowest standard on entrance.

" 4. Take the case of a draft of fifteen children from an efficient Infant School " into an Upper School. They have passed Standard I., and their work for the " next year is to pass Standard II. If the Teacher were unfettered by standards " some few of these scholars would be placed in the lowest class, but the greater " number would pass into Class III., and some would rapidly pass towards the " upper part of the school. But if the Standards are to be considered, with a view

The failure in writing and arithmetic above the Second Standard is especially remarkable, excepting only in the Sixth Standard in writing.* In its principal object, *viz.* a greater degree of proficiency in the three rudimentary subjects of instruction, the Revised Code has been followed by the injurious results which were predicted by its opponents. These results cannot have been clearly before the Committee of Council on Education, when they authorized the insertion of the following passage in their Report (in 1866–67, pp. xx., xxi.), though the latter

" to the earning of the largest Capitation Grant, all must stay in the lower part
" of the school, so as to pass in Standard II.
" 5. The fact is, that no two schools should really be judged by the same
" standard. The requirements which are absurdly below the proper mark in one
" school would be severe in another."
* Mr. Stewart (pp. 210-5) reports a general decline, throughout his district, not only in the extent of the subjects of instruction, but in the success with which the purely elementary ones are taught. The passage referred to is as follows:—Report of Comm. of Council on Education.—"The failures in the examination prescribed
" by the Revised Code have been consequently greater in 1866 than in 1865; and
" there are very few schools in which the old rate has been maintained.
" The extent to which schools are failing to prepare their children for this test
" may be seen at once by comparing the columns of figures in the following table,
" which represents the percentage of children presented for examination upon
" which annual grants have been paid in two successive years:—

No.	1865.	1866.	No.	1865.	1866.
	Per cent.	Per cent.		Per cent.	Per cent.
1	98	60	22	96	45
2	100	78	23	85	83
3	93	87	24	90	78
4	84	80	25	98	68
5	77	85	26	75	59
6	80	71	27	100	54
7	79	71	28	94	91
8	100	89	29	96	92
9	97	88	30	100	98
10	88	55	31	100	85
11	87	86	32	84	60
12	91	89	33	62	53
13	97	74	34	98	68
14	99	85	35	96	86
15	100	78	36	88	70
16	85	73	37	96	70
17	92	80	38	97	80
18	82	44	39	100	83
19	97	80	40	93	72
20	100	69	41	99	72
21	95	75			

"The falling off in the standard of the work done in these schools may, I
" think, be traced without much difficulty to the following causes:—
" 1. The employment of inferior teachers.
" 2. The reduction of the teaching staff in each school.
" 3. The employment of monitors instead of pupil-teachers."

portion of the paragraph points to one of the chief characteristics
of schools which earn the largest rate of grants under the Revised
Code:—" The Revised Code continues to answer the object of
" its authors by compelling teachers to attend to their scholars
" generally, and not mainly to the most clever or regular among
" them, as represented by the first class. The first class, no
" longer receiving the same attention as before, is often less
" good than it was ; and, *throughout the schools, the minimum*
" *which each child must learn, in order to pass for a Grant under*
" *Article* 48, *is apt to be of a mechanical character, and to efface*
" *that more intellectual aspect which, under the old system, struck*
" *a visitor looking at one of the best schools as a whole, rather than*
" *at each of its scholars.* So far as instructions could guard
" against this drawback, they were emphatically given by our
" predecessors on the occasion (September, 1862) of notifying
" the introduction of the Revised Code to Your Majesty's
" Inspectors."

When the light of the preceding table is thrown on the results of examination under each Standard in 1863 and in 1866,
the present condition of instruction in the rudiments will not be
found to justify the "*drawback*" which in guarded language is
here partially confessed.

The instructions referred to left the radical defect of the
method of inspection untouched. The separate examiners of
reading, writing, and arithmetic recommended by the Royal Commission have not been appointed. This examination has been
imposed on the Inspector, aided by an assistant, but as now employed, the time of the Inspector is exhausted in examining in
the three rudiments of learning. He has no opportunity for a
general survey of the organization and discipline—for the school
is not assembled in its classes, but re-arranged according to the
Standards of the Revised Code. He cannot ascertain the tone
and method of the religious teaching, nor test the general intelligence of the scholars by the skill of the first class in reading
with expression; nor in an understanding of what they have
read; nor in their proficiency in grammar, geography, or history, if he is previously to do the work assigned to him in pages
xx. and xxi. of the Instructions upon the administration of the
Revised Code* (Minutes of 1862–3). Mr. Cook is there reported

---

* The Rev. John Menet calls attention to the following effects of the Minute of
May 19, 1863, and to the contrast between that Minute and the Instructions of
September, 1862, sec. 7, p. ix. :—" The Minute of May 19, 1863 (see Postscript) has
" tied the Inspector's hands, by requiring that in all schools not examined for
" the first time, the Examination in the three subjects shall precede the Inspection
" properly so called. Any one who is interested in the subject will find some forcible

to have said that this examination required from four to six hours for 150 children. If, however (where there are two departments of schools), the merely mechanical work of mustering and registering the scholars in their Standards, and the testing of the reading, writing, and ciphering were confided to his assistant in one department, the Inspector might readily inspect another department in all the above-mentioned particulars. Then a second grant might be made, to depend partly "upon the school's " whole character and work," and partly upon the adequacy of the teaching staff, as suggested by the Royal Commission. There would then be a reason for "the inspection of each school by a " highly educated public officer," while the "general test" would be fortified by individual examination.*

" remarks upon it in the Report of M. Arnold, Esq., in the last Report of the Com-
" mittee of Council on Education (1863–4), pp. 186–189. The effect of this Minute
" in relation to schools under Uncertificated Teachers, as in all other schools, is to
" make it almost impossible for the Inspector to judge accurately of the general
" state of a school, and its value as a whole, in its ordinary daily working. Real
" inspection, with this end in view, is impossible after an examination for which
" the school has been broken up into the several standards, and by which both
" children and teachers are tired. Inspection is simply impossible under such
" circumstances.
" P.S. The following Statement will show how far the Revised Code and the
" Instructions of September, 1862, have been superseded by the Minute of May
" 19, 1863:—

Revised Code, Article 50, p. 7.	Instructions of September, 1862, Section 7.	Minute of May 19, 1863.	Remarks.
The Inspector does not proceed to examine scholars in reading, writing, and arithmetic, for the grant, until he has first ascertained that the state of the school does not require it to be withheld.	The grant to be made to each school depends, as it has ever done, upon the school's whole character and work. The grant is offered for attendance in a school with which the Inspector is satisfied. . . You will judge every school by the same standard that you have hitherto used as regards its religious, moral, and intellectual merits. The examination under Article 49 does not supersede this judgment but presupposes it. . . . It does not exclude the inspection of each school by a highly-educated public officer, but it fortifies this general test by individual examination.	To make it an instruction to the Inspectors to perform their duties in each school, not inspected for the first time, in the following order, viz.:— (a) Examination of the children in religious knowledge, where the Inspectors have to report upon it. (b) Examination in the subjects prescribed by the Revised Code. (c) General inspection of the school, allowing for previous acquaintance with it.	Column 3 contradicts columns 1 and 2, i. e. both the Revised Code and the Instructions of September, 1862. The Examination on which the Grant depends is begun and finished without an inquiry into the school's whole character and work. The Inspector does proceed to examine without first ascertaining the state of the school. Under Minute of May 19, Examination does supersede this judgment. Examination does practically exclude the inspection of each school by a highly-educated public officer. Examination does not fortify this test, for the test is practically done away with, and the grant settled by the Inspector or his deputy without it. The provisions of Revised Code that money should be paid only after due inquiry into the merits of each school are practically made void by Minute of May 19.

* The Royal Commissioners proposed that the examination in reading, writing, and arithmetic should be made by examiners appointed by the County Board,

The scholars fail to pass even the low Standards under the Revised Code, partly because the principal and assistant-teachers lose heart under their work. The methods by which the teaching of the rudiments is, in the best schools of Holland, Prussia, and Switzerland, refined and elevated above a mechanical drudgery are here generally falling into disuse, since the object of the schools has been contracted to those " results " which have been interpreted to be the goal fixed by the State for elementary education.

It will be found that the Committee of Council have not simplified the Administration of the Annual Grants. They will have to superadd the former inspection to the present mechanical examination.*

One of the objects proposed to be accomplished by the Revised Code was the simplification of the details of administration. If, however, this result may be tested by the ratio of the expense of office-work and of inspection to the average attendance of scholars in the aided and inspected schools, the commutation of the several grants to teachers into a Capitation Grant paid to the Managers has had little effect. The cost of the office administration alone was $6\frac{1}{4}d.$ in 1860, and $5\frac{3}{4}d.$ in 1866 ; and that of the office administration and inspection combined was 1s. $6\frac{1}{2}d.$ per scholar in 1860, and 1s. $6\frac{1}{4}d.$ in 1866.

The failure of the Revised Code to improve the rudimentary instruction in schools is not, however, solely due to the foregoing causes; it is, in a great degree, also to be attributed to the diminution of the number and the reduction of the skill of the teaching staff. The Committee of Council had found in those parts of Europe in which primary education had been successfully organized, that a fixed number of scholars, not to be exceeded, had been assigned to each teacher, and assistant or pupil teacher. They were thus led to conclude that, where a school had more than thirty scholars, the teacher should be aided by a pupil teacher. The Minutes of 1846 prescribed that " the number of pupil teachers apprenticed to any school" should " not exceed one to every twenty-five scholars ordinarily " attending." There is no allowance made in these Minutes for the numbers supposed to be taught by the principal teacher to qualify the foregoing maximum number of pupil teachers.

---

while the general Inspection continued to be conducted by H.M. Inspectors, and that an additional grant of 2s. 6d. a child on the average attendance should be given wherever the Pupil Teachers were in the proportion of one to every thirty scholars.

* Minutes, 1862–3, p. xviii., Instructions to Inspectors on Administration of Revised Code. This individual examination was contemplated in the Minute regulating the Capitation Grant of 1853.

Practically, the grants under these Minutes were intended to encourage the appointment of one pupil teacher to every twenty-five scholars after the first twenty-five ordinarily attending the school. The Revised Code seriously diminished these inducements.* The conditions of the Grant only stipulated that one pupil teacher should be employed for every forty scholars, or an assistant-master for every eighty scholars, in both cases after fifty scholars had been assigned to the principal teacher. So that the first eighty-nine scholars might be taught by one principal teacher without help, but every complete addition of forty scholars to the first fifty was to have the aid of one pupil teacher. The principal teacher was, under the Minutes of 1846, " to give " the pupil teachers instruction in the prescribed subjects during " one hour and a-half at least on five days in the week, either " before or after the usual hours of school-keeping." Under the Revised Code, these 7½ hours per week were reduced to 5—two of them may be given on the same day—and the pupil teachers may receive their instruction in the evening school, which was not previously permitted. Those only, who know what evening schools are, can estimate the fatally injurious influence of such an arrangement on the' instruction of pupil teachers.

The effect of recent changes is to confide the appropriation of the Capitation Grant under the Revised Code to the managers, with only minimum requirements as to pupil teachers. Have the managers, then, with a reduction of assistance maintained the previous relative number of pupil teachers and the efficiency of their education? The Royal Commissioners reported in 1861 that the pupil-teacher system was then, " on the whole, " excellent " (p. 106). They said, " It appears to be one of the " most important contributions made to popular education by " the administration of the Privy Council Grants " (p. 107).† By inspecting Table No. III. in the Appendix it will be seen that, in 1861, the average attendance of scholars in inspected schools for the year preceding the December 31, 1861, was 919,935, and that they were taught by 8,698 certificated teachers, 381 assistant, 491 probationary, and 16,277 pupil teachers. Reckoning each assistant and probationary teacher as equal to

---

* The condition (6) of clause 52 of the Revised Code is:—The Grant is reduced—

By sums of 10*l.* for every 40 or 80 after the first 50 of the average number of scholars in attendance, unless there be either one pupil teacher fulfilling the conditions of Articles 81-9 for every 40 scholars, or one certificated or assistant master fulfilling the conditions of Articles 67 and 91-3 respectively for every 80 scholars.

† They suggest for its improvement that the system should be graduated to the rate of wages in different parts of the country: that the labours imposed on pupil teachers, especially girls, should be reduced: and that some change should take place in the subjects of study, substituting English Literature and Physical Geography for one or two books of Euclid.

two pupil teachers, and assigning thirty scholars to the principal teacher, there was in 1861 one pupil teacher to every thirty-six scholars. Thus the Committee of Council had made a fair advance towards the accomplishment of their intention, that one pupil teacher should be employed for every twenty-five scholars. They had also educated a large body of teachers trained in colleges after five years' apprenticeship in schools. Moreover, up to 1860 the progress of extension proceeded *pari passu* with the supply of trained teachers and assistants. This co-ordination of the extension with the maintenance of the quality of education ceased with the Revised Code.

In 1866* an average of 1,082,055 scholars was taught by 12,179 principal, 1,061 assistant, and 10,971 pupil teachers, which, under the same conditions as before, shows a proportion of one pupil teacher to every 54 scholars. The Managers had, therefore, failed to keep up their teaching staff. Every pupil teacher had 18 more scholars to teach in 1866 than in 1861, though it is preposterous to conceive that a pupil teacher, even in the fifth year of his apprenticeship, could keep in order, much less teach, 54 scholars.† It is to be observed also that, though the number of schools under principal teachers had increased from 6,258 to 8,303, the number of pupil teachers had diminished by 5,306, or from 16,277 to 10,971.

If the Managers of Schools were so discouraged as to sanction this reduction, we may readily conceive that they might permit their interests and those of the schools to be sacrificed, by accepting the minimum of time for the instruction of pupil teachers in the Evening School, when, with reduced grants, they had to enter into fresh agreements for service with the principal teacher, and therefore, not seldom, to make injurious concessions. The interest of the master in carefully training and instructing the pupil teachers was diminished when the Government withdrew the direct annual payment to him for the discharge of that duty. Mr. Cowie (p. 398, Minutes, 1865–6) says :—" The schoolmaster also does not care to have pupil " teachers, because he gets no pay for teaching them." Again, " he has not only no inducement to bring forward boys as pupil " teachers, but positive inducements to keep them back." Moreover, the substitution of agreements liable to be dissolved by six months' notice for the indenture of five years' apprenticeship

---

* See Table No. III. in Appendix.

† It would be difficult to exaggerate the disorganizing influence of such a reduction of the staff of teachers in elementary schools, or the consternation with which this inevitable consequence of the Revised Code was foreseen by all qualified by experience to form an opinion as to the consequences of this administrative change.

rendered the relations of the pupil teacher and his master more uncertain, and, in many cases, weakened the pupil's motives for zealous application.*

Other causes have also been in operation to make the training of the pupil teachers less successful. The school has become a scene of mechanical drudgery, quite unlike the work of the best Swiss, Dutch, and Prussian Schools.† The substitution of monitors for pupil teachers down to the minimum requirements of the Code, has too often limited the aims of the school to the standard of rudiments which earn the Capitation Grant. Consequently, the daily work of the pupil teachers is of a humbler character, which—though not necessarily—has become less instructive in method. The pupil is discouraged and spends his life in a dull and mean routine, in which he has nothing but the rudiments to exercise his skill in teaching. The quality of the pupil teachers has consequently so grievously

---

* " The principal reduction continues to be in the number and quality, or " both, of male pupil teachers. This reduction is not due so much to deficiency " in the number admitted, as to removals in the course of apprenticeship. The " boys, as they grow up, are tempted with higher wages in other employments, " and the Managers are isposed to let them go as they become more expensive." —*Min. of C.*, p. ix., 1866–7.

The School Manager finds it unprofitable to compete with "the demand for " intelligent lads; he cannot give sufficiently high pay." (P. 398, 1865–6.)

† It has not been difficult (1) to improve the plans and internal construction of schools and the arrangement of their desks and classes; nor (2) to introduce a class-organization based on the principle of free individual progress, with such groups for collective instruction as are consistent with attention to the laggard and dull and with the recognition of personal merit; (3) nor to bring to the teacher's aid some of the best apparatus. (The system of *Standards* under the Revised Code tends to derange all this organization.) (4) The discipline has also been to a great extent based on a law of gentleness, and the teacher has been trained to despise an appeal to fear rather than to conscience. (5) But the part which the most refined methods of teaching play in making learning attractive to children, and thus securing a willing obedience, is not generally appreciated. Even many of the most able of the Principals of Training Colleges do not struggle against the extreme imperfection of the methods still in use in the instruction of infants and of the lower classes of the boys' and girls' schools. All that can here be said is, that the imitative faculties and the imagination, so strong in very young children, are too little employed; that the course of instruction is not delicately progressive; that the exaggerated methods of Pestalozzi have not passed through the alembic of a practical English mind, by which their subtleties might be exhaled and invaluable method remain; and in the higher classes, the methods of teaching Grammar, Geography, History, and even Arithmetic, cultivate the memory too much at the expense of the intelligence. This is not the place for further details. But those who are disposed to avail themselves of such excellent suggestions as are contained in Mr. Menet's 'Practical Hints on Teaching' (Bell & Daldy, 1867) will find that this Manual was intended for an organization of the school by *classes*, and not by *standards*, for the presence of a due proportion of well-instructed Pupil Teachers, and for the cultivation of the intelligence by graduated instruction—awakening the reason and appealing to the imagination; and not at all for a dull, mean, mechanical drill in the humblest elements of learning. Such methods as I found in 1839 in the Canton of Zurich, in the schools of Holland, and in some parts of Germany, could not co-exist with the Revised Code.

fallen off, that such Principals of Training Colleges as have had 19 years' experience find that the pupil teachers who now enter those institutions are approaching every year the low standard of the qualifications of the untrained candidates who formed the only sources of supply to Training Colleges before 1848.

The Royal Commissioners thus describe the contrast up to 1861 between pupil teachers and the untrained candidates for admission into Training Colleges:—" The utmost extent of the " attainments of the untrained students, on their admission to the " Training Colleges, was an imperfect acquaintance with reading, " writing, and arithmetic. The pupil teachers, on the other " hand, have furnished a constant and sufficient supply to all " the Training Colleges, and their acquirements and general " fitness for the posts for which they have been selected are best " attested by the fact, that only 12·68 per cent. of the total num- " ber admitted, are removed during their apprenticeship, either " by death, failure of health, failure in attainments, misconduct " or other causes, including the adoption of other pursuits in life.* " Considering the stringency of the tests applied to ascertain the " qualifications—moral and intellectual—of each individual in " every year of his apprenticeship, this is a most successful result." —(Report, p. 106.)

These are no longer the characteristics of the Pupil Teachers who seek to enter Training Colleges. Since the Revised Code, the deterioration of their qualifications has been so rapid that it was found necessary, at the Christmas examinations for admission into the Training Colleges in 1865 and 1866, to reduce the standard of attainments, in order to admit such numbers as might approach to the probable demand for Certificated Teachers in Schools.

Nevertheless, the discouragement to the choice of the teacher's profession as a career has been so great, that the number of students in the Training Colleges has steadily diminished since 1863. In December, 1862, there were 2,972, and at Christmas, 1863, a maximum of 3,109 students in the Colleges. But in 1866 there were only 2,403, or 706 fewer in three years.

According to returns moved for by Mr. Adderley (see Table

---

* Minutes, 1858–9, p. xxxii.

The Commissioners of Inquiry thus describe the pupils prior to the introduction of the Pupil-Teacher system:—" Most of the pupils on their entrance were " exceedingly ignorant. The reading of a few was good, and all read with fair " fluency, though seldom with correctness or 'good expression. The writing of " about half was good, of one-fourth inferior, and of the remaining one-fourth very " deficient. The arithmetic of about one-fourth was good as far as vulgar fractions, " about one-half could go as far as compound multiplication, whilst the remainder " were ignorant even of these rules. Most of them, however, had a considerable " knowledge of the Bible, derived principally from teaching at Sunday Schools." —*Report*, p. 112.

No. IV.), 2,513 Candidates presented themselves for examination at the Training Colleges at Christmas, 1862, of whom 1,983 passed, and 1,755 entered in 1863. Whereas at Christmas, 1866, only 1,584 Candidates were examined, of whom only 1,207 passed, and 1,121 entered the Colleges in 1867. At Christmas, 1867, the Candidates were only 1,478 in number, of whom 1,160 passed; and of these last 963 had been Pupil Teachers.* This failure in the supply of well-trained Pupil Teachers to the Colleges is a grievous discouragement to institutions which are indispensable to the maintenance of an adequate supply of efficient teachers. This blow has fallen on them after an outlay of 308,010l. by the subscribers on the buildings, which was met by grants of 137,967l. from the Government, or, together, after an expenditure of 445,977l.† Though the Training Colleges have accommodation for 2,471 resident‡ students, they contained only 1,922 in February, 1867. Their income was 133,113l. in 1863, and only 102,693l. in 1866, owing to the withdrawal of Parliamentary aid.§

Regarding the diminution of the supply of Candidates, abstractly from the deterioration of their qualifications, Mr. Cowie says—" At present, the number of youths who apply for admis-
" sion to Training Colleges has been diminishing yearly. I
" give the numbers which relate to the 14 schools which I have
" inspected. This looks as if the current had set strongly in
" one direction. I see but slender probability of its changing
" at present" (p. 399). Again (p. 400, in 1865-6)—" If the
" Managing Committees of Training Colleges ' cannot' secure
" competent Teachers for ' school managers' from the want of
" persons to train for the office of teacher, all they can claim
" from the Committee of Council seems to be, *that the regula-*
" *tions shall be revised which have cut off the supply of students;*
" and *if, from other causes, this cannot be done effectually, the*
" *establishments must be either permanently or temporarily con-*
" *tracted, and perhaps some closed."* The founders of Training Colleges will scarcely regard this catastrophe with so much complacency.

Mr. Cowie reports, in 1866-7 (p. 396), that " two Colleges—
" Highbury and Chichester—have been given up."

But in 1865-6, Mr. Cowie states (p. 397) that " the waste

---

* I am informed that only 224 male candidates passed for Church of England Colleges. St. Mark's College had 52 of these, and Battersea College 40, leaving only 132 to be divided among all the other Colleges in England and Wales. This is a disastrous result.
† See Minutes, 1866–67, p. 370.
‡ " In the Presbyterian Scotch Colleges the students, with the exception of a " small part of the females, are not boarded in Colleges, but provide their own " lodgings."—*Minutes,* 1866-7, p. xi.
§ See Table VI. in Appendix.

" of teachers is assumed to be about 7 per cent.—*i.e.* of the whole
" number now employed, it may be conjectured that 7 per cent.
" will, in the course of 1866, leave the profession either by death
" or by change of occupation.   To supply this waste, taking the
" number of certificated male teachers at about 6,300, about 440
" would be required to fill up vacancies, and therefore the num-
" ber of new schools which would be supplied would be *nil;*
" whereas, it will appear, that a considerable number of new
" schools were placed under inspection in 1865."   Again, in
1866–7 (p. 395):—" The extension of the ' system of education '
" which is so loudly called for, is impossible without a ready
" supply of teachers.   Schoolmasters are not to be had.   If we
" scarcely make good the annual waste, to talk of extension is
" out of the question."

   " The quality of the young men now under training in point
" of intelligence and culture, compared with their predecessors of
" some years back, has," Mr. Cowie says (p. 394, 1866–7), " been
" generally noticed in unfavourable contrast."   The circumstances which have operated injuriously on the education of
Pupil-Teacher candidates have been explained.   " The reduc-
" tion of the minimum requirements which took place soon after
" the Revised Code was passed " is, according to Mr. Cowie
(p. 394), " by some considered a cause of deterioration in the
" class of certificated teachers."   There were two motives
alleged for this reduction.   One was, as Mr. Cowie intimates
(see p. 394, Min., 1866–7), to bring the salaries of masters
within the range of the resources of schools ; the other, to faci-
litate the introduction of masters with lower stipends to apathetic
and rural districts.

   The first of these objects could not be admitted as a motive
of public policy, unless we were to adopt the maxim of certain
American school managers, who are reported by Mr. Fraser
to say, " that the cheapest schoolmaster is the best."   It is
obvious that the standard of the elementary education, in a
great country, ought not to depend on the intelligence, disposi-
tion, or resources of such local managers.

   The second object, as is shown in the Report of the Committee
of Council for 1866–7 (pp. xii., xiii., xiv.), was rather, to a great
extent, to be met by increasing the supply of mistresses for
mixed schools, in small rural parishes.   But it should not be
forgotten, that Mr. Matthew Arnold reports that in Prussia the
qualifications of a Teacher in any district in which there is only
a primary, and not a superior school, are required to be higher
than where both exist.

   If the qualifications of the Candidate Pupil Teachers on
entering the Training Colleges had been kept up, these expe-

dients might have rendered the reduction of the minimum requirements for teachers' certificates (of which Mr. Cowie speaks) as unjustifiable as they were injurious. As it is, a lower kind of teacher has been trained, in numbers so diminished as to be unequal to more than the annual waste. " The failure in the supply of trained teachers is a very great " blow to the maintenance of the Certificate ; for the increasing " difficulty of finding suitable persons to fill vacancies in schools " will add to the number of those who are opposed to the condi- " tion of the Certificate."—(Cowie, p. 395, 1866–7.)

The Committee of Council had intended, by the Minutes of 1846, to create and sustain a scheme of education for teachers equal to that possessed by any other country. The plan of the apprenticeship and Training Colleges obtained the deliberate approbation of the Royal Commission in 1861, and the " nine " years' training of teachers—five as Pupil Teachers, two at the " Normal School, and two years under Probation,"—appeared to Mr. Fraser especially to excite admiration in America (p. 50, Mr. Fraser's Report). The existence of this system has been endangered by the Revised Code, because its efficiency has been impaired. The whole scheme originated with the Government, and was by them proposed to Parliament. The Managers of Schools were encouraged to adopt it by direct grants. Whatever extension took place in our elementary school system, and whatever degree of efficiency it attained, were the immediate offspring of the Minutes of 1846. The period of failure and decline dated from the substitution of the Capitation Grant of the Revised Code, with its conditions, for the grants under these Minutes. That change has proved that the voluntary zeal of the Managers of Schools had already been loaded with burthens which it was scarcely able to bear, and that it could not supply the amount of money grants withdrawn, nor fulfil much beyond the minimum conditions on which these grants were administered under the Revised Code. The whole system of public aid has thus been shaken to its very centre—the Managers of Schools have been discouraged—the emoluments of the teacher have been lessened, and his hopes disappointed. Pupil teachers are therefore scarce, and are easily attracted to other employment. Their education is not well cared for, because it has ceased to be the interest of the principal teacher; their qualifications at the end of their five years' engagement are much lower than formerly. The Training Colleges have an insufficient supply of inferior students, who pass a lower examination for their certificates, but, even though thus imperfectly qualified, they are not trained in greater numbers than are required to supply the annual waste. The extension even of a deteriorated system of instruction is impeded by the effect of the Revised Code in discouraging the apprenticeship, and the supply of Students to Training Colleges.

Grave changes made in the character of the inspection have not secured the expected improvement of the scholars in the knowledge of the three rudiments. The inspection has been converted into a mechanical examination of these rudiments, contrary to the suggestions of the Royal Commission, who intended that the examination in these subjects should be conducted by separate officers.* The attention of the Managers and Teachers has, by the conditions of the Capitation Grant, been injuriously concentrated on a routine of daily drill in reading, writing, and ciphering. The result has been a larger amount of failures among the scholars when examined in these subjects, and the general neglect of the higher subjects of instruction, and of cultivation of the general intelligence of the children. The schools are lower in their aims, the scholars worse instructed, and there is a tendency to deterioration in the whole machinery of education.

The Revised Code has constructed nothing; it has only pulled down. It has not simplified the administration. It did not pretend to accelerate the rate of building schools, or to improve their structure. It has not promoted the more rapid diffusion of annual grants and inspection to the apathetic parts of cities, or the founding of schools in small parishes and for the sparse population of rural districts. It has generally discouraged all instruction above the elements and failed in teaching them. It has disorganized and threatens to destroy the whole system of training teachers and providing an efficient machinery of instruction for schools. These ruins are its only monuments. It has not succeeded in being efficient, but it is not even cheap; for it wastes the public money without producing the results which were declared to be its main object.

This analysis of the disorganizing tendencies of the Revised Code has been a painful but necessary duty, because the machinery of Training Colleges, Teachers, and Pupil Teachers created by the Minutes of 1846 must be regarded, not merely in its existing relations to the denominational system in co-operation with the State, but as a means of supplying that teaching staff without which no system of education can exist. To impair or to destroy this is therefore a blow, not only to the denominational system of schools, but to any scheme of national educa-

---

* I should prefer that the present Inspectors should be responsible for both examination and for inspection, and that their reports should be so ordered that they could not neglect either duty.

tion, for none can exist without competent teachers, and it would not be an easy task to replace the Training Colleges now existing.

Some other indications may likewise be gathered from the effects of the Revised Code which it may be desirable to note.

Up to 1861–2 progress had been made to a great extent, attained by the action of the Government, in forming public opinion—stimulating local activity, guiding this by means of inspection and by the conditions of aid, and sustaining local exertions by proportionate assistance. The Revised Code may, from one point of view, be considered as an effort on the part of the Government to withdraw from this position of active sympathy and consequent responsibility, in the hope and expectation of thereby evoking a greater amount of local activity. Bearing in mind that the local initiative never had been assumed by the Government, the Revised Code has settled the question whether the Committee of Council can shift on to the local managers a greater share of the annual charge for the support of schools, and whether the regulations ensuring the efficiency of schools can be safely relaxed. It has clearly established the principle that whatever power be delegated to local authorities, and whatever discretion be confided to the School Managers, the standard of elementary education will not be maintained, unless the Committee of Council on Education make this its chief and immediate concern, and frame the conditions of its Grants in aid of Schools so as to ensure this result. This conclusion implies the primary necessity of the maintenance of a Central Inspection, and of aid from the Parliamentary Grant.

It is clear that the Education Department had been in advance of public opinion as to the outlay required for the efficiency of schools; as to the number and skill of the teaching staff; and as to the nature of the instruction. When the amount of aid was reduced, and the conditions of the grants were relaxed, local intelligence and zeal failed to keep up the efficiency of the schools. If, therefore, the Committee of Council have not intended to supersede the existing denominational system by some other, they must bear in mind that, before the Revised Code, the strain on the local exertions and contributions was as great as could be borne—and that the appeal to local intelligence and zeal for greater sacrifices has failed. Apparently this conviction has at length established itself in the Education Department.

The Committee of Council have recently adopted a Minute, the intention of which is to prevent the further reduction of the number of the Pupil Teachers and the neglect of their education. But I fear that the Minute is so complicated, and the interest which the Managers have in availing themselves of it is so

obscure, that it will have little, if any, effect.   Before, however,
describing simpler and more efficacious expedients, it is desirable
that the provisions of this Minute should be explained.

In their Minutes of 1866–7 (p. x.) the Committee show that
the loss of Pupil Teachers annually increases during the term
of their engagement.   The table given exhibits the following
progressively greater deficiency in each year:—

	2nd Year.	3rd Year.	4th Year.	5th Year.
Males	43	93	130	145
Females	*	63	79	199

The whole loss during the five years of apprenticeship was 752
in 11,221 pupil teachers.   " It was to check this falling away
" in the most valuable years of service, that the third and fourth
" paragraphs of the Minute of 20th February, 1867, were framed."
" The effect of this Minute is that a male pupil teacher who gets
" to the middle of his apprenticeship represents an extra grant
" of 5*l*., 10*l*., 13*l*., 15*l*., or 18*l*. to his school if he completes his
" apprenticeship, and gains admission into a Training College,
" the amount varying according to the proficiency which he has
" acquired and maintains.   If it were not for the increasing ex-
" pense of the pupil teachers as they grow older, the managers and
" principal teachers of schools have every motive to retain them
" because their efficiency in upholding discipline and imparting
" instruction, being much greater than that of novices, tends to
" produce a better and more agreeable school, and to qualify it
" for a larger grant by passing more of its children.   The extra
" grant offered by the Minute comes in aid of the increasing
" expense of the later years of the pupil teacher's service, and
" we entertain a confident hope that the prospect of obtaining
" a share of it will help to retain apprentices in their schools,
" and to stimulate both them and their masters in vigorously
" applying themselves to the lessons out of school-hours whereby
" those prizes are to be earned."

It is, however, clear that these results will not be obtained
unless the managers, either voluntarily or in obedience to regulation, require that the pupil teachers shall receive one hour and
a half of instruction daily—not in the evening school—nor unless
the master obtain a separate remuneration dependent upon the
success of the pupil teachers.

Another part of the Minute of the 20th of February, 1867,
encourages an increase of the number of Pupil Teachers by
"an additional grant of 1*s*. 4*d*. per pass in reading, writing,
" and arithmetic up to a sum not exceeding 8*l*. for any one
" school (Department)," on certain conditions specified.

---

* In this year there is an apparent gain of 181, who entered on their engagement by passing the examination of the second year.

This Minute is intended to correct acknowledged defects which threaten the efficiency, if not the existence, both of the Pupil-Teacher system, and of the Training Colleges. The improvement, thus introduced, is in the right direction, but this Minute ought to be stripped of technicalities,—the limitations on the grants ought to be less restricted, and the encouragement, both to the teachers and managers, more certain, obvious, and direct.

I have already expressed my opinion that the individual examination should be regarded as superadded to the general Inspection which preceded the Revised Code. This combination was intended by the Minute of 1853, relating to the Capitation Grant of that date. The individual examination might be chiefly confided to the assistant, under the occasional superintendence of the Inspector, while he inspected a separate department of the same group of schools. The grant contemplated under the Minute of Feb. 20th, 1867, but with a higher rate of aid, should be given, without any complicated conditions, on proof of efficiency of instruction in the higher subjects, and on condition of the employment of one pupil teacher for every 25 or 30 scholars after the first 25.

This cursory notice of a mode of adjusting the Capitation Grant so as to supply the Managers with motives to maintain in efficiency the teaching machinery of the schools and the higher subjects of instruction, may for the present suffice. It will receive more detailed attention in a subsequent part of this Memorandum.

Among the objects which the Royal Commissioners sought to accomplish, was to render the present system "applicable to the " poorer, no less than the richer, districts throughout the whole " country" (p. 328). They estimated that, " in round numbers, " the annual grants in 1860 promoted the education of 920,000 " children, whilst they left unaffected the education of 1,250,000 " others of the same class" (p. 83). The number of aided Day School groups inspected in the year ending Aug. 31st, 1866, was 8,049, with 12,504 Departments or schools, and an average attendance of 1,048,403 scholars, while there were 1,510,871 on the books, and 1,234,491 were present at the examination. The school-rooms could accommodate 1,668,294 scholars, at eight square feet of superficial area for each child.

It is not my intention to attempt an exhaustive estimate of the number of children taught only in unaided schools, or receiving little or no education.

The number in 1866 whose education is affected by aided schools may be fairly reckoned by the attendance on the day of examination, or 1,234,491. These scholars form a very large proportion of those attending the schools supported by religious denominations, which, according to the Commissioners, amounted in 1860 to 1,549,312 children. Besides these, there were 43,098 scholars taught in schools not specially connected with religious denominations :—47,748 in schools supported by taxation, and 35,000 in collegiate, superior, or richer endowed schools. They further concluded that 860,304 scholars were taught in private schools, one-third of whom belonged to the upper and middle classes : leaving 573,536 who are children of the classes usually educated in primary schools. Satisfactory means to arrive at similar exhaustive statistics in 1867 do not exist. But we may fairly conclude that at least 350,000 children attend unaided denominational primary day-schools, and 600,000 are in elementary private schools, or nearly one million of children are in schools of the same class as those aided, but which receive no assistance from the annual grants. In the uninspected schools, the education generally obtained is of a much inferior character to that given in the schools aided by the public grants. The number of children who obtain no education either in denominational, or public, or private schools, or whose education is limited to so short a time, and is so meagre, as to be almost worthless, is probably very great.

It would, therefore, probably be a fair estimate of the present state of the education of the manual labour class if we were to reckon 1,250,000 to be on the average in attendance on aided and inspected day-schools. But that their attendance is often so irregular, so rapidly intermittent, and so capriciously changed from school to school, as to minimize the advantages which such children might otherwise derive from the most efficient class of existing day-schools. Some of these evils can only be corrected by the growth of a sense of parental obligation as to the education of children. They certainly are not to be cured at once by a compulsory system of school attendance which no vigilance could enforce on migratory and apathetic parents. Then we may safely reckon that at least one million of children are in unaided and uninspected schools. These scholars are subject to all the hindrances affecting the improvement of the class just described, and to the further grave disadvantages of attendance at schools of an exceedingly inferior type—in which, at best, only a very imperfect acquaintance with the rudiments could be obtained. We should thus account for 2,250,000 children out of upwards of 3,500,000*—if we were sanguine enough

---

* This estimate is obtained by adding six years' increase to the population, as ascertained at the last census—the increase being supposed to be at the same rate as in the last decennial period, or 1·19 per cent. per annum.

to adopt the Prussian standard of one-sixth. After due allowance for the children belonging to the middle and upper classes,
and for those in various ways now educated at the public
expense, according to the estimate of the Royal Commission,
it is at least clear that there are always many children who are
of school age and not at work, but who are in no schools at all.*
The inquiries of the Committee of the Manchester and
Salford Education Bill in 1851–2, and of the Manchester Education Aid Society, and the Diocesan Board of London, in 1865–6,
disclose a condition of ignorance and apathy among the poorest
portion of great cities which requires some heroic remedy.

Various causes have combined to retard the growth of the
denominational system. It has failed to satisfy the wants of
the poorest districts of large cities and of remote rural districts.
Where the sensuality, indigence, or apathy of the parents is
greatest, the zeal of the religious bodies has encountered a task
beyond its strength. Those who would promote popular education on account of its social and political bearing, demand that
opportunity should be given to the national forces outside the
pale of the religious organization, at least so far as to enable
municipal and other bodies to contribute to the annual resources
of the schools—to found more schools in neglected districts—
and to provide for their support. Meanwhile, the Government,
by a wise extension of the principle of the Factories' Regulation
Acts, has rendered the provision of the means of education
necessary to the successful working of the new Acts.†
It may therefore be expedient first to examine the obstacles
to the extension of the present denominational system, aided by
the Parliamentary Grants.
Some of these obstacles are giving way before the gradual
influence of time and experience. In an address delivered at a
Meeting of the Congregational Union of England and Wales,
at Manchester, on Friday, October 11th, 1867, Mr. Baines, the
member for Leeds, avowed a complete change in his own opinion,
and that of a large part of the Congregational Communions, as
to the scruples which had prevented their accepting aid for their
schools from the Government Grants, and had made them earnest
and persevering opponents of the interference of the State in
public education. He urged that the Congregationalists should
seek to be admitted to participate in the school grants, without

---

* Since the above estimate was in type, I have received from an able member
of the Manchester Education Bill Committee the results of an exhaustive local inquiry in two wards of that city, which I print in Appendix IX.
† See, in Appendix No. VIII., abstract of recent legislation—communicated by
Mr. Redgrave, H.M. Inspector of Factories.

any such condition as to the constitution, government, instruction, or inspection of their schools as would imply that the Government were cognizant of a religious element in them. They would then accept aid, and admit lay inspection, and comply with all the administrative conditions solely as means of promoting the efficiency of the secular instruction, which, with a view to political and social improvements, they regard as a legitimate object of the State.

I attach great value to this adhesion, for, in the first place, the Congregationalists number 5,500 congregations, above half-a-million communicants, and assemble, in 5,000 Sunday-schools, more than half-a-million scholars.* None of these communions have yet devoted much of their energy to the founding of day-schools, but their contributions to missionary enterprise show what sacrifices they are capable of making for any cause which deeply stirs their sympathies and awakens their zeal.

Their congregations contain many of the most intelligent and wealthy of the middle classes, whose influence was severely felt by the Government of Sir Robert Peel, in 1842, in the defeat of the education clauses of Sir James Graham's Factory Regulation Bill. But their congregations are also, both in the great towns and in villages and remote hamlets, often the missionaries of the manual-labour class. Some consist almost exclusively of artisans, and others contain a large proportion among their communicants.

Many of the less known sects will follow the lead of the Congregationalists. The Primitive Methodists have 3,118 chapels, besides 3,192 places rented for Divine worship. Their communicants number 135,247 ; they have 2,934 Sunday-schools, in which they teach 234,794 scholars. Their congregations consist almost solely of humble tradesmen, and families supported by manual labour. The amount of the contributions of factory hands, colliers, quarrymen, masons, and other handicraftsmen, in their sects, towards the building of their chapels and Sunday-schools, is very remarkable.

Thus the admission of the Congregationalist Dissenters to the benefit of the school grants is not an insignificant event. It points also to the early co-operation of the humbler sects of Dissenters which are mainly composed of the religious portion of the manual-labour class.

Through the position which the deacons and class-leaders of such congregations will come to hold in the Committees of the

---

* The following statistics of the Baptist Denomination are extracted from their 'Handbook for 1868.' In Great Britain there were 2610 chapels, 2381 "churches" (*i. e.* organized religious congregations), 220,163 " members," *i.e.* communicants, and 191,551 Sunday scholars.

day-schools, parents of the manual-labour class will be more fully awakened to a concern for the education of their children. They will more and more desire to assist in superintending it, and they will make sacrifices proving the sense they have of parental obligation.*

Whatever may ultimately be the result of the co-operation of the Congregationalists and other communions with the Government, it is obvious that the progress must be gradual. The charge of an efficient day-school will greatly increase the burthens which these congregations have to bear. The annual cost of the education of each scholar is about 30s., and of this outlay 12s. were in 1860 provided by Government Grants. If this rate of aid were renewed, 18s. per head would remain as a charge on local resources. Of this, a larger part would be derived from school-pence in the day-schools of these sects than in other schools. If the weekly pence averaged 3d. per scholar, 12s. per annum might be derived from this source, leaving 6s. to be subscribed by the congregation.

The obstacles to the founding of day-schools by these religious bodies have hitherto been twofold. The day-school has not formed, so distinctly as the Sunday-school, a part of their conception of the accessories of a religious congregation. In the humbler of these communions, the outlay on their chapels and on the support of their ministers has absorbed their resources

---

* The small proportion which the school-pence bear to the whole income of primary schools is a sign of the small interest which the parents take in the education of their children. They have little opportunity of forming an intelligent interest. They are seldom present at the Inspector's visit or invited to any genuine examination of the school, or even to a display of the children's acquirements. Few persons have had the foresight which Dr. Temple showed when he proposed that the parents should select a certain number from their body to act on the School Committee. (There would be no difficulty in finding sagacious and thoughtful parents to co-operate as managers on the School Committee in the manufacturing districts, nor in those agricultural parishes in which the farmers and tradesmen send their children to the parochial school. Where the school is attended only by the children of rural labourers, it is to be feared that such representation would at present be useless.) The parents can select the school, when the opportunity for choice exists, and can withdraw their child—if not required by the factory law to send him as the condition of his employment to the only existing school. But when these things have been taken into consideration, is it uncharitable to say, that families which earn from 30s. to 60s., or 6s. per head weekly, on the average of the entire factory population of the cotton and woollen districts, ought to make greater sacrifices than an average payment of 2½d. per week, or 10s. a-year, for each child's education? If they paid more, their right in the management of the school would become more apparent. The present meagre payment is the ground from which, with greater intelligence and virtue, they will step into the discharge of the parental right to, at least, assist in regulating their children's education.

On the other hand, if the time should come when the political relations of primary education rise into a clearer light, the school-rates which reach the labourer's or artisan's cottage, would remind him that this tax is collected for the education of his child, and inspire him, if he be a worthy and intelligent man, with a desire personally to aid in securing its efficiency.

They have had scruples which prevented their accepting Government aid, and without that assistance they were unable to establish schools which could hope to compete with the aided schools. If they are now to succeed, they will owe that success —as the Wesleyans do—to the income which they will obtain from school-pence, unless they also obtain aid from local rates.

But threepence per week will only be paid by the most thoughtful and prudent of the manual-labour class. Below that class stagnate the lees of the city population, which missionary zeal itself cannot reach.

But it is not only in cities that the system of Parliamentary Grants to the schools of the religious communions finds limits. There are, everywhere, districts in which the zeal that has created the denominational system is languid. The non-residence of proprietors—the indifference of the residents—the smallness of parishes, the sparsity of the population have been truly enumerated as reasons for this apathy. But the principle on which the present system rests, could only procure the completion of the whole fabric of national education, within that time to which the political wants of the nation now point, if the Government were clothed with the power of the initiative, and if the rate of public grants were considerably increased. There remains the obvious expedient, suggested in 1852–3, and renewed in the Bill which Mr. Bruce introduced in the last session, of awakening the municipal spirit and power in aid of the voluntary zeal which has created the denominational system.

When the Government, by the Minutes of 1846, entered vigorously into co-operation with the religious communions, it had determined, after seven years of trial, that no other principle than that of religious zeal could then be relied upon for the promotion of popular education. There were no signs that public opinion had been aroused to a sense of the political importance of the education of the manual-labour class. The Town Councils had only languidly, and by no means generally, availed themselves of such powers as those conferred on them by Mr. Ewart's Free Libraries Act. The measure, carried through Parliament by the present Speaker of the House of Commons, permitting Boards of Guardians to pay, from the poor-rates, the school-pence of children of outdoor paupers, has, even to this day, been almost everywhere neglected. Boards of Guardians have been, step by step, induced to make the education of pauper children in workhouses fairly efficient, but only since Sir Robert Peel provided, by a public grant, for the salaries of teachers in workhouse schools.

It may be doubted whether, even if extensive powers, such as those contemplated by the Manchester and Salford Education Bill of 1852, or Lord Russell's Boroughs Bill of 1853, had been then conferred on Town Councils without the obligation of carrying them into execution, the rate-payers and the municipal bodies had at that time attained so thorough a conviction of the nature and extent of the measures necessary to secure the education of the neglected classes, that such measures would have been at once carried out, except in the great centres of manufacturing and commercial activity. It is even now questionable whether if the same principle of a local rate in aid of the denominational system—now embodied in the Bill introduced last session by Mr. Bruce, Mr. Forster, and Mr. Algernon Egerton—be adopted, merely permissive powers will have much effect. It may rather be expedient to render the adoption of the Act a matter of discretion with the Privy Council.

While therefore the analysis of these proposals is reserved for a later portion of this Memorandum, it is expedient here to consider the means by which the present system can be enabled to overflow its apparent limits. Happily, all plans for deriving aid from local rates contemplate the support of the existing system of denominational schools, and propose to incorporate the authority and regulations of the Committee of Privy Council.

The Royal Commission reported * " that the small parishes " are, in most respects, in a less advantageous position with " regard to education than the large ones. It is certain they " have, in point of fact, far less availed themselves of the " Government assistance; and the proof of this is, that the " average numbers in uninspected schools are 34, those in in- " spected schools are 75. If we wanted further evidence, it would " be found in the conditions of the schools, as they have been " recently described, in different parts of the country. In the " Diocese of Oxford, out of 339 parishes, with a population " below 600, and containing a population of 125,000, only 24 " schools two years since (1858) were in receipt of Government " aid; in Herefordshire, out of 130 parishes with a similar " population, only five received such aid; in Somerset, out of " 280 such parishes, only one; in Devon, out of 245, only two; " in Dorset, out of 179, ten; in Cornwall, out of 71, one; and " in the Archdeaconry of Coventry, Birmingham excepted, out " of 76, seven. And these facts become more significant if we " bear in mind the large proportion of schools in parishes, whose " population exceeds 600, which have connected themselves with " the Committee of Council. 'If we look,' says Mr. Nash

* P. 317-318.

" Stephenson, 'at the average of all parishes over 600 that are
" ' under inspection, we shall find it to be 1 in 2·97 ; and if
" ' we look at the average of all parishes under 600, we shall
" ' find it only to reach 1 in 26·44.' "

Since the Royal Commission reported, progress has been
made in the building of Schools and the extension of annual
grants · in these small parishes, but the general complexion
of the facts remains unchanged. The number of Poor-Law
Districts in England and Wales containing above 500 inhabitants is 6,619, and of these 4,204, or nearly two-thirds,
contain schools aided by annual grants, whereas the Poor-Law
Districts containing less than 500 inhabitants numbered 8,219,
of which 7,295 districts, with a population of 1,772,276, and
563,849 children of school age, received no aid from annual
grants, or only one in about nine of these small districts
obtained such assistance.

The Duke of Marlborough, in the House of Lords, called
attention to the fact that these parochial divisions for poor
relief are not ecclesiastical parishes or school districts. "While
" in the public return the unaided parishes are stated at 11,024,
" the real number of school parishes unaided is 8,866. And
" when we come to the parishes with less than 500 population,
" where the greatest amount of destitution is felt, we find, that
" whereas the Poor-Law parishes unaided having a population
" under 500 amount to 7,996, the school parishes unaided with
" a population under 500 amount to 5,392. That was the state
" of things in 1863–4 ; but in 1866, to which year the Report
" of the Committee of Council now on the Table reaches, I find,
" ' that the total number of Poor-Law parishes unaided has been
" ' reduced from 11,024 to 10,404; and giving the same pro-
" ' portion of difference between the Poor-Law parishes and the
" ' school parishes, the entire number of unaided parishes is
" ' 8,368.' "

Mr. Warburton* reported to the Royal Commission that out
of 159 schools in parishes having less than 500 inhabitants in
Wiltshire, only nine were then in receipt of annual grants. "In
" stating these facts,† indeed," say the Commissioners, "we
" must remember to take into account that a number of these
" parishes, probably amounting to 15 per cent., possess each a
" population of less than 100, and therefore could scarcely
" support any school beyond a Dame's School." In 1866–7 the
Committee of Council report,‡ that out of 8,219 Poor-Law
Districts with less than 500 inhabitants, 1,783 had less than

---

* P. 318.   † P. 318.   ‡ P. cix.

100, and 3,923 less than 200, while 5,641 had less than 300 inhabitants.*

Among the obstacles to the extension of Government aid, therefore, is the smallness of the population of many of the rural districts. Before examining the nature of these obstacles, it may be well to call to mind that many of these small parishes contain schools. Mr. Bellairs reports, that in his district, out of a total of 429 schools, there are 141 aided and 288 unaided. Among the schools thus without grants are not a few founded by proprietors or other wealthy inhabitants, or by clergy, who are unwilling to accept aid or admit inspection. Of such schools some are comparatively efficient. But when all such schools are enumerated, there still remains a large class of unaided schools, respecting which the Royal Commissioners report, " Mr. Fraser, who has not been sparing in his strictures " on the shortcomings of many assisted schools, states† broadly " ' that it seems impossible to bring a school into a good state of " ' efficiency unless the managers avail themselves to the fullest " ' extent—particularly in the employment of pupil teachers— " ' of the resources offered by the Committee of Privy Council. " ' I only met with two exceptions to this rule.' Mr. Wilkinson " sums up his examination of the state of education in the " schools in the conclusion‡ that ' the degree of efficiency of " ' inspected schools is very much greater than that of schools " ' which are not inspected,' while of 35 witnesses whom he " examined, 33 answered in favour of inspected schools. Mr. " Winder says as explicitly, ' the best public inspected schools " ' achieve, I suppose, something like the maximum of success " ' possible under the present conditions of attendance;' adding, " ' No unassisted public school, and no private school under " ' circumstances which admit of a fair comparison, could com- " ' pare with the best assisted schools, but the indifferent " ' assisted schools are no better than those which are un- " ' assisted.' Mr. Hare, speaking§ of the great seaport towns " on the East of England, tells us that ' none of the unassisted " ' schools in Hull, excepting the Boys' British School, will " ' bear comparison with the assisted schools.' And finally, " Mr. Cumin speaks in similar terms of the western seaports, " Bristol and Plymouth. He says,‖ ' The private scholars " ' whom I did examine were very inferior to the best public

---

* The distribution is as follows:—Number of Poor-Law Districts having between 400 and 500 inhabitants, 1,140; between 300 and 400 inhabitants, 1,438; between 200 and 300 inhabitants, 1,718; between 100 and 200 inhabitants, 2,140; less than 100 inhabitants, 1,783. Total, 8,219 Poor-Law Districts.

† Report, p. 277.   ‡ P. 277.   § P. 277.   ‖ P. 278.

" ' scholars. At Bristol . . . I found only one good public
" ' school which was conducted by voluntary efforts alone.' "

The extension of the annual grants and of inspection to the
unaided school districts is therefore desirable. The Royal
Commissioners reported, in 1860, that * "The unassisted public
" schools are far more numerous than those which are assisted,
" amounting to 15,952 schools, exclusive of 115 factory schools,
" containing 17,000 scholars, whereas the assisted public schools
" are only 6,897. They are inferior, however, in the number of
" the scholars; those on the books of the assisted public schools
" being 917,255, those on the books of the 15,952 unassisted
" public schools, only 654,393. Some of these schools are
" unassisted, because the managers or patrons reject assistance,
" either from religious scruples, or because their patrons dislike
" interference. These obstacles, however, are comparatively
" rare, and are rapidly diminishing. The great cause which
" deprives schools of Government assistance is their non-per-
" formance of the conditions on which that assistance is offered,
" a non-fulfilment of which the principal causes are poverty,
" smallness of population, indifference, or, as it has been lately
" called, apathy." Since the Report of the Commission, the
number of assisted and inspected schools had risen, in 1866, to
8,303, and the number of scholars present on the day of examination to 1,234,491, while accommodation was provided in the
schools (at 8 square feet per child) for 1,688,294 scholars.

But the question how the denominational system aided by
public grants can be extended so as to provide for the education
of the lowest classes of the great cities, and for the population
of the small and apathetic parishes, has not been solved by the
degree of advance made in the last seven years. To the condition of these unaided parishes, Mr. Walter has perseveringly
called the attention of Parliament and the public.

The object to be obtained is twofold. *First*, to raise the
efficiency of the unaided schools at least to the level of those
which receive assistance and are inspected. Mr. Fraser points
out the conditions indispensable to this result. Then *secondly*, to
found schools where they do not exist, and to evoke the local
resources necessary to meet the public grants.

The Committee of Council, in their Report for 1866–7, p. xii.,
point out the way in which many of the unaided small parishes
might comply with the conditions of the present Minutes by
placing mixed schools in charge of a mistress. They estimate†

---

* P. 278.
† See in Appendix Extract from pp. xii., xiii., xiv. of the Report of the Committee of Council on Education, 1866–7

the annual outlay in such a school for 60 or 70 children at 67*l*., —certainly at too low a rate—and show that half that expenditure might be obtained from the Government grants. The passage is quoted in the Appendix in order that the whole details may be examined. By the introduction of mistresses trained at Hockerill, the greater part of the small parishes of Hertfordshire,* and of other neighbouring districts, have thus been enabled to participate in the public grants. And there can be no doubt that such arrangements afford great facilities for the support of most useful schools.

Miss Burdett Coutts has also proposed a plan, now successfully in operation in several districts, by which a group of schools in a district of small parishes may be organized, taught, and visited by an ambulatory teacher holding a certificate. The Minutes admitting these schools to the benefits of grants need simplification, and the removal of some restrictions.† If these changes were made, it is probable that this plan would be much more generally adopted.

---

* The progress of the settlement of Certificated Teachers in Hertfordshire was as follows in each succeeding year. In August, 1857, there were 55 Certificated Teachers in this county; in 1858, 65. On December 31, 1859, there were 75; in 1860, 88; in 1861, 93; in 1862, 105. In 1855 Certificated Teachers were employed in only 22 parishes in Hertfordshire, whereas in 1861 there were at least 67 parishes employing them. The following list illustrates the operation of this system:—

Schools in Rural Districts to which Hockerill Students have been appointed in Parishes under 1000 Population.

Hunsdon, Herts	516	Thornhaugh, Northampton ..	243
Albany, Ditto	700	Calmworth, Beds	527
Furneaux Pelham, Ditto	620	Berden, Essex	414
Ickleford, Ditto	546	Stilton, Hunts	724
Arton, Hunts	311	Sandon, Essex	771
Farnham, Essex..	556	Kilshall, Herts	318
Foxearth, Ditto	400	Great Parndon, Essex	491
Yeldham, Ditto	696	Teversham, Cambridge	231
Bayford, Herts	297	Dunton, Beds	518
Tetworth, Beds	416	Sutton, Suffolk	618
Clothall, Herts	492	Seer Green, Bucks	334
Hertingfordbury, Ditto	799	Hazlemere, Ditto	996
Datchworth, Ditto	635	Hyde, Herts	419
Flitwick, Beds	773	Kingsey, Bucks	237
Comberton, Cambridge	562	Hadham, Little	884
Herongate, Essex	475	Heveningham, Suffolk	354
Bramfield, Herts	191	Pulloxhill, Beds	704
Sandon, Ditto	771	Latimer, Herts	244
Heath, Beds	953	Witchford, Cambridge	559
Birchanger, Essex	358	Elyworth, Hunts	787
Sedgeford, Norfolk	742	Greenstead, Essex	789
St. Ippolyts, Herts	952	Litlington, Cambridge	693

† Among these restrictions are Sections (*b*) and (*c*), Article 135. Code of 1866–67, p. lxxxvi., Minutes.

Mr. Walter, however, contends for the adoption of a proposal which has probably been misunderstood. He seeks the extension of public grants to schools not taught by certificated teachers. He has been understood to contend that, as the principle regulating the distribution of Government grants is, under the Revised Code, "*payment for results*," equity requires that the production of those results should, without other conditions, establish a valid claim for all the aid granted to other schools. I do not conceive that this has ever been Mr. Walter's intention; but, on the other hand, he does not appear to have defined the conditions and limits of this aid to schools taught by uncertificated teachers.

The misconceptions grounded on the popular view of the Capitation Grant under the Revised Code have been mischievous. According to these misconceptions, the Government have defined the "*results*" for which they will make grants to be a certain standard of attainment in reading, writing, and arithmetic. The intention of the interference of the State, by means of inspection and pecuniary aid, is satisfied when these "*results*" are attained. If this were literally true, then the production of *the* "*results*," however brought about, would constitute an equitable claim to the whole of the Government assistance. But we have seen that these "*results*" have never been any other than the *minimum of the amount of instruction* sought by the State, and that instruction is only a part of the civilizing influence of a school. The Government grants have not been given to secure the power to read, write, and cipher only, but by means of certificated teachers, and a certain proportion of pupil teachers, to attain higher "*results.*" Though too much reliance has been placed on the zeal and intelligence of the local managers to secure the highest results, by keeping the teaching staff of the schools in a state of efficiency, it is not to be conceived that the Government deliberately adopted the conclusion that the " be all and the end all " of primary instruction was such a proficiency in reading, writing, and arithmetic as is defined in the Standards of the Examination under the Revised Code. Mr. Lowe speaking on the introduction of the Revised Code said, " We fix a minimum of education, " not a maximum. We propose to give no grant for the attend- " ance of children at school unless they can read, write, and " cipher; but we do not say that they shall learn no more. " We do not object to any amount of learning." *

Nevertheless, the neglect to adopt the recommendation of the Royal Commissioners, as to the means by which an examination in the three rudiments should be conducted—separately from

---

* ' Hansard,' pp. 237-8, vol. clxv.

the general inspection of the school—the omission of a separate Capitation Grant for the maintenance of a sufficient staff of pupil teachers—and the absence of any grant to encourage the higher forms of instruction, have given rise to the mischievous popular impression that the whole object of Government aid is the attainment of a certain meagre proficiency in reading, writing, and arithmetic; for which "*results*" "*payment*" is made. No severer condemnation of the Revised Code could be uttered if this were true. But it is by no means true. The grants under the Revised Code are also given, as we have said, for the maintenance of a machinery by which higher results may be attained. This would have been clearer if it had been declared that the annual grant given on the average attendance of the scholars was specially intended for the maintenance of a trained teaching staff in proportion to the number of the scholars. A large part of the evils might have been avoided if the following rates and classes of Capitation Grant had been adopted and their objects declared.

The aid of the Committee of Council might have been divided into the four following forms of Capitation Grant, *viz.* :—

1. A Capitation Grant of five shillings* for every child who had attended more than 200 meetings of the school in the preceding year, and had passed an examination (conducted by special examiners) in reading, writing, and arithmetic — one shilling and eightpence being deducted for failure in each of these subjects.

2. A Capitation Grant of five shillings per head on the average attendance in the preceding year in all schools in which the buildings and arrangement of the desks were approved—the apparatus and books were declared to be sufficient, and, besides a certificated teacher, one pupil teacher for every 40 scholars after the first 30 was employed.†

---

* The Capitation Grant which correspondes to this in the Revised Code is eight shillings, subject, in like manner, to a deduction of one-third for every child who fails to pass either in reading, writing, or arithmetic, according to the standard of the Code (Article 48). The reason for reducing the amount of 'the grant, de-pendent on this examination, from 8s. to 5s., consists in the fundamental objections to this mode of testing the work done in a school (*vide* ante, p. 15) and arises out of all the injurious consequences which have been proved to have followed these Articles of the Revised Code.

† The average per scholar of grants for Certificated, Assistant, Probationary, as well as Pupil Teachers in the year ending 31st December, 1861, was 10s. 5d., and the average of grants for Pupil Teachers alone was 6s. 11¼d. per scholar. In the Clauses 2 and 3 in the text, it is proposed ₜto restore 9s., to be appropriated to the maintenance of the Staff of principal and assistant teachers in schools. The reasons for this form the substance of the argument in the preceding pages. It remains to be remarked, that by dividing this 9s. into two Capitation Grants, with more stringent conditions for the second, opportunity is afforded for the play of the discretion of the Managers. If (under Clause 2) they prefer to have one Principal

3. An additional Capitation Grant of four shillings in schools in which one pupil teacher for every 30 scholars after the first 25 was employed.

4. A further grant of four shillings for every scholar who should succeed to the satisfaction of the Inspector in a graduated examination in any two of the following subjects, *viz.:* in grammar, English history, geography, book-keeping, or vocal music.

Among the subordinate conditions of the second and third forms of the Capitation Grant should be regulations as to the teaching of the apprentices, and a conditional payment to the principal teacher for such services. The other conditions should be as simple as possible.

If the principles and arrangements of such a Minute had been adopted, instead of those of the Revised Code, the average rate of aid would not have exceeded that granted in 1860, *viz.*: 12*s.* per head on the average attendance of the scholars,* and its maximum might have been limited to the 15*s.* proposed by the Royal Commission. The managers would probably have had sufficient inducements to maintain a due proportion between the number of the teachers and pupil teachers, and the scholars. The instruction of the apprentices would have been properly cared for; the supply of pupil teachers to the Training Colleges would have been maintained; and the mischievous popular interpretation of the phrase "*payment for results*" would not have practically reduced the level of elementary education to a meagre standard of proficiency in reading, writing, and arithmetic. Moreover, the first form of aid for the attainment of the minimum results of instruction might have been extended to schools not having certificated teachers, during a period of transition extending over two years.†

Teacher for the first thirty scholars, and one Pupil Teacher only for every succeeding forty, they will earn only five shillings. If, on the contrary, they appoint one Principal Teacher for the first twenty-five scholars, and one Pupil Teacher also for every succeeding thirty scholars, they will earn nine shillings, or one shilling and fivepence per head less than under the old Code.

* This calculation is made on the presumption : *first,* that three-fourths of the scholars would earn the first grant. Less than two-fifths earn that form of capitation grant now. The grant under the first head would be three and ninepence on the average. *Secondly,* all schools would probably earn the next five shillings. *Thirdly,* probably half the schools would earn the next four shillings, or the average would be two shillings. *Fourthly,* certainly not one-third of the scholars would earn the grant under the fourth form. The average would therefore be 1*s.* 4*d.* These several grants would amount to 12*s.* 1*d.*

† I am reminded of a similar provision which existed in Mr. Adderley's Minute of July 26th, 1858, and which was incorporated in Article 143 of the first Code, but has disappeared from the Revised Code. By this Minute and Article students who had passed the examination for certificates might receive, but only in their first engagements after leaving the Training School, a stipend of 25*l.* per annum

Whatever steps be taken to bring the spirit and power of local or municipal government and the resource of local rates in aid of elementary education, the same necessity will exist—as we have previously urged—for the maintenance of the regulations of the Privy Council as to the character, capacity, knowledge and skill of the teacher, and of the proportion of the teaching staff to the number of the scholars. It is for this reason that we have painfully analyzed the consequences of the Revised Code, which first relaxed the conditions of public aid. We have shown that the tendency of the local management is, with such relaxation, to introduce inferior teachers—a smaller staff—and a lower standard of training for pupil teachers and of instruction for scholars. In like manner, any relaxation of the conditions of the public grants, or of the aid from local rates as to the certificate, would cause the introduction of ill-taught, unskilled teachers, for whose life and character there would be no sufficient guarantee.

The entire public service—civil, military, and naval—has, of late years, taken precautions to ensure the competency of its servants, both by initiatory and competitive examinations, which, in several departments, are repeated at each step of promotion. The same principle pervades the learned professions, and every year adds to the stringency of the examinations and regulations which determine what previous education, what learning, and what proofs of reputable life shall be required, both from those who are entrusted with public duties, and from those who have to do the work of professions in which the interests of the public require the greatest learning and skill. So it will be found that wherever, from elementary education, Governments have reaped truly national advantages, they have taken the most jealous precautions that the teaching of youth shall be confided to none, with the sanction and aid of the State, who have not given proofs of character, learning, and skill.

---

if males, or of 20*l.* if females, instead of the ordinary augmentation, provided that they were employed in a rural school, (*a*) not containing more than 1,200 square feet of superficial area in the whole of its school-rooms and class-rooms, or (*b*) which could be certified as not needing, nor likely to be attended by, more than 100 scholars.

This payment was made for two years only.

II. Teachers working under these regulations were exactly in the same position as students working under the usual provisions of the Minutes.

1. They were inspected and reported on exactly in the usual manner.

2. They might receive their parchment certificate at the end of two years under the usual conditions.

3. They might have Pupil Teachers and receive the gratuity for instructing them.

4. The only difference was that for two years they received a sum instead of augmentation, and at the end of the two years, if they had two favourable reports, they received their augmentation according to the class of their certificate.

Such a system is consistent with complete liberty of teaching. There is no monopoly of instruction in Great Britain. It is free to all religious communions, to every political party, to every form of social organization. Any one may become a teacher. Any one may obtain a certificate by passing the requisite examination. With a certificate, any one may derive whatever advantage the State confers on schools taught by competent persons. What is denied is, that it is for the interest of the country that the standard of instruction, by which the aid of the State can be obtained, shall be determined by local managers rather than by Parliament, moved to action by the Education Department.

The report of Mr. Fraser on America is full of proofs that the local management in the United States cannot be depended upon to fulfil any of the requirements of the law. It often chooses the cheapest schoolmaster as the best, it provides unsuitable buildings and meagre apparatus. It keeps open the school no longer than the allowance from the State fund will provide for its maintenance. It is satisfied with almost any "*results.*" On the other hand, the Reports on Prussia, Switzerland, and Holland, by Mr. Matthew Arnold and the Rev. M. Pattison on the state of elementary education in Germany, give abundant evidence of the remarkable results obtained, when the State—jealous of the public interest—requires that sufficient proof of ability, knowledge, and skill, shall be given by everyone who has charge of the education of youth.*

Nor can inspection, however conducted, supply the place of the certificate. An individual examination of the scholars may determine whether they can read, write, and cipher, but even in this, an examiner may be greatly deceived by a teacher who is an adept in special preparation. But no inspection can ascertain the relative merits of schools in all that relates to the moral

---

* On this subject, the following authorities may be consulted. See particularly Vol. IV. of 'Report of Education Commission,' p. 72, "the indispensable guarantee " of a certificate of capacity, without which, in France, no man may teach."

"Teachers must be certified, and their examination for the certificate is con- " ducted by the Central Board of Public Instruction."—*Report on Education in the French Cantons of Switzerland,* page 124.

"The law of 1806 was very short and simple. It adopted the existing schools; " but it did two things which no other school-law had yet done, and which were the " foundations of its eminent success; it established a thorough system of inspection " for the schools, a thorough system of examination for the teachers.'—Page 149.

"The certificates of morality and capacity are still demanded" (*i.e.* by the law of 1857) "of each teacher, public or private."—*Report of M. Arnold, Esq., on Schools in Holland,* page 149.

"In no State can a person, unprovided with a certificate of fitness, be appointed " master of, or teach in any primary school, whether public or private . . . . . " This is not a recent institution anywhere."—*Rev. M. Pattison's Report on Education in Germany,* page 244.

discipline—the order springing from a willing and intelligent obedience—the power of thought which is awakened only by the skill of a trained teacher, and all the other effects of those forms of teaching which alone civilize. For these "results" there is no test. Yet these are not only the most valuable, but they are the results without which all mere attainments are valueless. Dr. Temple, in his evidence before Sir John Pakington's Committee, insists with great vigour that, for such results, the certificate is a guarantee much higher than any inspection.

So also as to character. To have been five years an apprenticed pupil teacher, whose whole conduct was under the eye of the teacher and the clergyman,—to have passed, every year, a stringent examination and obtained certificates of good conduct, —to have entered a training college, after a searching examination, and to have pursued studies in it for two years—passing a further examination at the end of each year,—all this training under vigilant guardianship affords a warrant for reliance on character which the conduct of the teachers so educated has justified. No sufficient substitute has been proposed for this prolonged trial of character and conduct.

If the bare unqualified proposition of reducing all aid to a "*payment for results*" (so called) and determining the amount simply by examination were adopted, any cunning adventurer who could cloak the shame of a misspent life might set up an "adven-"ture" school anywhere in rivalry with the parochial, and earn, by success in drilling children in the three rudiments, the aid of the Government as a schoolmaster. Thus the support and implied sanction of the Government might come in aid of a parochial nuisance, perhaps introduced designedly to worry the proprietor or clergyman. And the education of the children might be confided to the care of a man in the secret practice of low vices, of no faith, disloyal, or corrupt.

The Committee of Council report (1866–7, p. 5) that the salaries of uncertificated teachers are about one-third lower than the certificated, but as a salary of 40*l*. to 45*l*. will secure the services of a certificated mistress, and 60*l*. to 85*l*. those of a certificated master, it is clear that the stipends cannot be reduced by the competition of uncertificated teachers without a further, and perhaps a fatal, discouragement to pupil teachers to enter this profession.

The immediate consequences of such discouragement would be felt in the Training Colleges. The resort to them for two years' training would rapidly come to an end. Moreover, the change would remove the motives which, under the existing Minutes, have induced uncertificated teachers in charge of schools to prepare themselves for examination for certificates.

The clergy often aid their studies, and with such encouragement 1,486 teachers between 1862 and 1866 presented themselves for examination, and 1,093 obtained certificates.

On these various grounds, the extension of the Capitation Grant on equal terms to schools, whether taught by certificated teachers or not, would not simply be a waste of public money, but would undermine and soon destroy the whole system of training by which the certificated teachers and the apprenticed pupil teachers now employed have been brought into the public service. Instead of so mischievous a waste of the public resources, it would seem better to withdraw public aid altogether, and to leave all schools solely to the support which can be derived from purely local agencies.

It is not conceived that the object which Mr. Walter had in view was that which has here been thus objected to. Much more probably it was the extension of such aid as would enable rural schools to avail themselves of the benefits of inspection, and to raise themselves to the level of a full participation of the benefits of aid from the Parliamentary Grant. The managers of a school might declare their intention either to prepare their teachers for examination, or within a limited period to obtain a certificated teacher. The school would then be inspected,— they would receive the aid and advice of the Inspector as to the steps which they had to take. Meanwhile, and during two succeeding years, the scholars would be examined individually in reading, writing, and arithmetic, and the school would receive aid under the first form of the Capitation Grant above described, according to the degree of the success of the scholars in each of the three rudiments. If, after the lapse of two years, the Managers failed to appoint a certificated teacher, the grant would be withdrawn.

But these expedients for the extension of the existing system of public grants and inspection into the districts into which it has not penetrated, depend on the power of the religious communions to co-operate successfully. Now it is clear that unless authority to take the initiative be conferred on the Committee of Council, much time must elapse before any such extension can occur as will satisfy the political wants of the country.

From his lucid and able address on Primary and Classical Education, delivered last November in Edinburgh, Mr. Lowe would thus cut the knot of these difficulties :—" I would say, " commence a survey, and report upon Great Britain parish by " parish ; report to the Privy Council in London the educational " wants in each parish, the number of schools, the number of " children, and what is wanted to be done in order to place within

" the reach of the people of that parish a sufficient amount of
" education. When that has been done, I think it should be the
" duty of the Privy Council to give notice to that parish that they
" should found a school, or whatever may be wanted for the
" purposes of that parish. If the parish found a school, then it
" would be the duty of the Privy Council to assist it, and that in
" the same way as it assists the schools already in existence. I
" would say, in passing, that I do not think we should disturb the
" schools already existing, except that they must submit to unde-
" nominational inspection, and to a conscience clause. If the
" parish does not agree to what is done, then I think there ought
" to be power vested in the Privy Council, or the Secretary of
" State, or some other great responsible public officer, to make a
" compulsory rate on them to found that school. I think the
" schools they found should be entitled to the same inspection
" and examination as the schools already in existence, and
" receive the same grants for results. That simple machinery
" would, in a short time, alter the whole face of the question,
" and place education within the reach of every one of Her
" Majesty's subjects."

Parliament would probably not confer such power on the
Privy Council Committee. But it may be well worthy of consideration whether the Privy Council should not, in concert with an
intelligent District Board, have authority to act after due inquiry
and report. The co-operation of the Central with a Provincial
Board in this initiative would be more in harmony with our English ideas of government. Such co-operation would be founded
on the appeal for interference from an intelligent and influential
minority in the district, and would not take place until after
due inquiry and report, nor without a well-ascertained and
sufficient amount of local concurrence. When these had first
been obtained, Mr. Lowe's proposal to confide the power of
initiatory action to the Government might be co-ordinated with
that of an intelligent minority. But Mr. Lowe has not said from
what sources he would derive the income of the schools thus built.
In the present inspected schools, 18s. 6d. are voluntarily provided from local sources to meet the 8s. 6d. per head from public
grants. Of this, in rural districts, from 6s. to 8s. consist of school-
pence. Probably, where the remaining ten or twelve shillings
were not spontaneously subscribed, Mr. Lowe would also charge
this part of the income on the local rates. In that case,
more than one-third of the annual school expenditure would be
derived from local, and less than one-third from general taxation,
and about one-fourth from school-pence. There would remain
the critical question of the constitution and management of the
chools thus founded, and their relations to the Committee of

Council on Education as to examination, inspection, and the conditions of the public grants. All these are the subjects of such anxious vigilance, that the financial features of such a plan present the least of the difficulties to be surmounted. On the other hand, Mr. Lowe has, with characteristic clearness and vigour, pointed to the need of a greater power in the Government to take the initiatory steps.

In order to apply to popular education the aid, spirit, and power which have, in the municipalities, effected so much for the improvement of our borough towns, Lord Russell introduced,* in 1853, his Borough Schools Education Bill. This measure proceeded, in a great degree, upon the results of the investigations of the local Committee which had prepared the Manchester and Salford Education Bill, and the general principles of both these measures are now revived in the Bill introduced in the last session of Parliament by Mr. Bruce, Mr. Forster, and Mr. Algernon Egerton.

Both Lord Russell's and the Manchester Bill were intended for the support of the denominational system of schools. Both left the management in the hands of the present school committees, without reserving any power of interference with the organization, discipline, or instruction of the schools, otherwise than by inspection. Both left unchanged the general inspection and the grants of the Committee of Council, with its authority to alter the conditions of its grants. The Town Council Education Committee had power to appoint local inspectors to observe that the conditions of aid from the borough rates were fulfilled. These conditions secured the right of parents to select the school in which their children should be educated, and to withdraw them from any instruction of which they disapproved on religious grounds. But the Manchester and Salford Bill intended to make this education *free from charge* to the parents; and provided fivepence per week for boys, and fourpence per week for girls and infants, to meet the Government grants, which amounted to threepence per week—thus superseding subscriptions and school-pence. †On the other hand, Lord Russell's Bill provided, from the borough rates, twopence per week to meet threepence per week, which were still to be derived from subscriptions and school-pence, and threepence per week from the grants of the Committee of Council on Education. Both contemplated an outlay of 8*d.* per week, or 32*s.* for 48 weeks' schooling, on the average attendance of the scholars.

---

* See volume 'On Public Education,' Longman, 1853, pp. 313 to 321.
† 'Public Education,' pp. 314 to 318.

These measures differed in other very important particulars. The Manchester and Salford Bill was intended for those two great boroughs alone. Lord Russell's Bill might be adopted in any corporate town, but not in other urban, nor in any rural districts. In the former Bill, provision was made, after due notice, and in default of the action of any voluntary assistance, for the building of schools in those districts of the two boroughs which were found to need them. This involved the difficult question of the constitution and management of schools founded by the municipality. In Lord Russell's Bill, no such power was given, and the erection of new schools was left to spontaneous agencies. Therefore, the aid granted under the latter Bill was to be confined to schools whose constitution had already been recognized by the Committee of Privy Council.

Similar principles are embodied in the Bill of Mr. Bruce, Mr. Forster, and Mr. Algernon Egerton. This measure has also been prepared in concert with a Committee on Education sitting in Manchester. The programme issued by that Committee describes its provisions in the following general terms :—

" The Bill is permissive in its character, and when passed it may " be adopted by the Rate-payers in any borough or district. When " so adopted, it places the administration of the funds in the hands of " a School Committee, elected by the Town Council in Municipal " Boroughs, and by the Rate-payers in other districts, who have power " to call upon the Overseers, or other Local Authority, to levy a rate " for Educational purposes.

" It adopts existing Schools as the basis of its operation, and only " contemplates the establishment of new Schools on the failure of " voluntary effort to supply, after due notice, any deficiency of school " accommodation.

" Trustees or Managers may, under the provisions of the Bill, " place their Schools in union with the School Committee, either as " Free Schools, or Aided Schools, and receive payment per head for " the attendance of the scholars on compliance with such conditions " as will secure the efficiency of the Schools, and protect the " rights of conscience ; but without the School Committee acquiring " thereby any right to interfere with the internal management, disci- " pline, or instruction in such Schools, otherwise than to see that the " conditions of Union are complied with by the Managers, and thus " what is commonly called the religious difficulty is entirely avoided.

" The principle of the Bill is Local Rating, for the support of " Free and Aided Schools, with Local Administration of the funds : " Union of existing Schools, without interference in their internal " management ; and security for the rights of conscience, without " violating the convictions of School Managers ; a power of appeal " being given in all cases to the Queen in Council."

This Bill also proposes to extend the same principle of aid

from the local rates from Boroughs (to which Lord Russell's
Bill was confined) to the rural districts. The education may
be either free from charge to the scholars, or the weekly school
fee may amount to any charge not exceeding ninepence. The
allowance to a free school is to be from fourpence to sixpence
per week, according to the age and sex of the scholar; or ninepence per week, when some trade, business, or manual occupation
is taught. But where school-pence are paid, they must equal
the amount of assistance from the rate. One-third of the
resources of the " aided schools" would therefore be derived from
school-pence, one-third from local rates, and one-third from the
grants of the Committee of Council on Education. The schools
would be independent of local subscriptions.

When the Education Committee, created by this Bill, are of
opinion that any part of their district is not sufficiently provided
with schools conducted in accordance with the conditions and
regulations, they may publish a report stating the amount and
description of the additional school accommodation required.
Within sixty days, any persons may then undertake to provide
for the need, and the Committee may accept an undertaking to
that effect. But if no such agreement is entered into, the Education Committee of the District may proceed to lease or purchase
land, and to erect such school-buildings as are needed. The
schools, so built, are to be conducted by the School Committee
as " free schools," or as " aided schools," under the general conditions and regulations; or the District Committee may, from
time to time, delegate such control and management—with or
without conditions or restrictions—to a body of Managers duly
qualified.

The same general intention pervades these three measures.
Their principal and common object is to bring the aid of
resources, derived from local rates, in support of the annual
expenditure of the schools founded by the religious communions.
The two later measures preserve the income derived from
school-pence, but the Bill of last Session would make the schools
independent of subscriptions.* All require the introduction of a

---

* The necessity of providing some other source for the income of schools,
besides the Privy Council grants and the local voluntary agencies, and the school-
pence, has long been apparent to those who apprehended that some measure like
the Revised Code would otherwise be adopted to restrain the growth of the Parliamentary Grant. This was one of the motives for the labours of the Committee
which framed the Manchester and Salford Education Bill in 1851—the responsibility
of all whose proceedings I gladly and fully partook. The necessity of providing
some initiatory power to found schools in the neglected districts, and to improve
such as exist though unaided, justifies an appeal to the local and provincial spirit
to aid voluntary religious zeal and the central action of the Government. But, in
all these proposals, it ought to be borne in mind that to the extent to which the
public charge is placed on the local rates it is a tax on a more limited area of

conscience clause, and reserve the right of examination by local inspectors. The three measures also concur in placing under the authority of the Education Department the regulations which determine the Standard of popular education, as maintained by the character and number of the teachers, and the provisions respecting the training of apprentices and teachers.

This is not the place in which to enter into a critical examination of the machinery by which it is proposed that this general scheme of a rate in aid of existing schools is proposed to be carried into execution.

It may, however, be remarked, that Lord Russell's Bill sought to avoid awakening alarm among the supporters of the denominational system, by limiting to one-fourth the proportion of income to be derived from the local rates, and by omitting all provisions as to the building of new schools in neglected and apathetic districts. By thus reducing to a minimum the amount of interference, it was hoped that the support of the religious communions might be more readily obtained.

Fifteen years have now elapsed since Lord Russell's Bill was laid on the table of the House of Commons. The Report of the Royal Commission, and the experience of the comparatively slow growth of the denominational system, aided only by public grants, have now revived, in a similar form, the proposals for aid from local rates made in 1852–53. There is, however, now a more general sense of the political necessity that Parliament should make adequate provision for the education of the people. This conviction is so strong, that the passage of some such measure for education in borough towns as that introduced last session by Mr. Bruce, Mr. Forster, and Mr. Algernon Egerton is likely to obtain an early and attentive consideration from Parliament.

The provisions for the extension of the powers given in this Bill to the rural districts will, however, require re-consideration. That which has to be chiefly borne in mind in such revision is,

---

assessment. This is one of the reasons why, in Lord Russell's Boroughs Education Bill, the burthen on the local rates was not allowed to exceed *one-fourth* of the whole estimated outlay. In my letter to Lord Granville, dated April 24th, 1861 (see 'Four Periods of Education,' Longmans, p. 559), I represented that this local rating should in no degree affect the proportion of the charge on the Consolidated Fund. For it would in that case be " *a removal of a charge* " " *from* " *an area of* 550,000,000l. *to one of* 86,000,000l." The proportions in Lord Russell's Bill of the three sources of the income of schools were:—one-third from the Parliamentary Grant; one-fourth (or 6s. 8d.) from the local rates; and the rest (10s. 8d.) from voluntary agencies and school-pence. These last would thus be relieved, and, the Privy Council Grants remaining without any change in their relative proportion, a charge on the Consolidated Fund would be more extensively diffused.

that in order that any such measure should pass through Parliament, it should be clear—

1. That the education committee of the district (whether a Poor-Law Union or other group of parishes) will represent intelligence and property. The provisions for its appointment should be far less complicated than those in the Bill of last Session. The selection and appointment of the District Education Committee by the votes of the whole body of rate-payers in a parochial union appears a very questionable means of securing a committee representing the intelligence of the union. If this District Education Committee were to partake with the Privy Council the authority of the initiative, such power could only be confided to men qualified by position, education, and experience for the discharge of difficult and important public duties.

2. That the schools to be built in the numerous small rural parishes will bear a constitution resembling those now aided, or such as may be recognized by future Minutes of the Committee of Council on Education.

3. That the local managing committee, of schools built by funds derived chiefly from the rates, will not represent simply the rate-payers, who will probably adopt too low and meagre a standard of instruction. The constitution of English society requires that the clergy, and the resident proprietors, as well as rate-payers and parents, should be members of this managing committee. The power of the rate-payers to appoint the managing committee should therefore be confined to a selection in certain proportions from these representative classes.

4. In those rural parishes in which the wages of labour are low, the district education committee might remit the school-pence, and require that two-thirds of the school income should be derived from the rates. But one-third should still assume the form of weekly pence paid from the rates on behalf of poor parents. It would thus represent the parental obligation unfulfilled on account of indigence.

5. It is very difficult to conceive that *"free schools"* (*i.e.* schools in which no school-pence are paid) and *"aided schools"* (in which school-pence are paid) could work side by side. The adoption of the idea of *"free schools"* has in part arisen from the desire to provide education for the children of indigent, sensual, or apathetic parents. These classes are essentially paupers as respects the education of their children. The faults or misfortunes of the parents may entitle them to the same aid in discharge of their parental obligation to *educate* as in that of their duty to *feed and clothe* them. But the distinction between the unfortunate or thriftless classes and the independent labourer should not be lost. The Guardians of the

Poor are now enabled, by Mr. Denison's Act, to pay the school-pence of the children of pauper parents; but perhaps the time is come when, as a condition of out-door relief, the education of every child, not at work, should be required, and made an imperative charge on the poor-rates.

6. The amount to be raised in each parish for the support of a school should be determined by the district education committee, and not by the parochial school committee.

There are also certain general considerations which apply equally to urban and to rural districts.

The establishment of free schools—as proposed in the Bill of 1867—or schools in which no school-pence will be paid, appears very questionable. To confound the obligations of the parent with those of the citizen is dangerous. The parent is not simply a rate-payer, having a right to claim education for a child whom it is the interest of the community to train for the discharge of future social duties. He has also a personal obligation, out of which springs his right to choose the school for his child, and his claim to be represented in the Managing Committee. He cannot neglect to fulfil the obligation without weakening, if not abandoning, this claim. But it is the interest of the State to strengthen every moral tie which unites families.

We owe to Mr. Walpole the extension of the principle of the Factories Regulation Acts to almost all forms of manual labour, excepting agricultural. The law now interferes to enforce the parental obligation to provide education for children, by making the fulfilment of it a condition of the employment of children for wages. It is lamentable that the ignorance and apathy of portions of the population should render this necessary; and it is greatly to be regretted that only, at the best, *half-time instruction* is secured for children in the associated employments affected by these Acts, and, in some of them, much less than half-time. There is, on account of the necessarily imperfect*

---

* Much industry has been expended on the advocacy of the doctrine, that *as much* or *even more* can be taught in the *half-time* which the law secures for factory-children, than in the *full time* of schooling enjoyed by children whose parents enable them to attend school both in the morning and the afternoon of every day. A very simple test is sufficient to expose this fallacy. In a factory district, schools generally contain both *half-time* and *full-time* scholars. In proportion to the number of the half-time scholars, the organization and instruction of the classes become more and more difficult. Full-time scholars, therefore, *cæteris paribus*, make most progress in a school in which there are no half-time children. But, notwithstanding the hindrance thus created to the success of the education of full-time scholars in a mixed school, the following result is always disclosed by an impartial inquiry. In a group of six or ten schools in which the half-time children amount to at least one-third, and do not exceed one-half the number of scholars, the full-time children will be found, at similar ages and after a corresponding number of days of school attendance, higher in the classes than the half-time scholars; and the half-time children will be found gravitating towards the lower

instruction of half-time scholars, a strong reason for raising to 14 the age to which these Acts extend their protection. One other form of legal compulsion is an obvious consequence of these recent Acts. It will be easy to define the circumstances in which the education of children, not at work, shall be made a condition of out-door relief. In order that the extent to which education is now made obligatory by law may be understood, I have printed in the Appendix* a memorandum, with which Mr. Redgrave has furnished me, describing the progress and present state of legislation on these subjects. From this it will be seen how important is the advance made in the Session of 1867, and to what extent the fact, that education is now a condition of employment for wages in almost all excepting farming occupations, necessitates the completion of our national-school system. The extension to agricultural districts of the principles of Mr. Walpole's recent comprehensive legislation may present difficulties, but none of them are insurmountable. And the founding and support of schools in the small and apathetic parishes is the obvious concomitant of such legislation.

The proportions of the school income which are to be derived, in urban and rural districts respectively, from the three sources proposed in the rate-in-aid Bill, deserve attentive consideration. The maintenance of the authority of the Committee of Managers is allied to that of the claim of the parents for representation on the School Committee. To merge both of these in the power of the rate-payers to elect a School Committee would be a rash change, likely to be followed by the withdrawal of the support of the religious communions from the schools, and would probably be fatal to the quality and character of the education given. On these accounts Lord Russell's Boroughs Education Bill provided that only one-fourth of the income of schools should be derived from local rates, while it proceeded on the expectation that three-eighths would be granted by the Privy Council Committee, leaving three-eighths to be furnished from school-pence and voluntary agencies. This limitation of the income to be derived from local rates might interfere with the rate of progress in founding schools in neglected districts. In such cases, the District Education Committee might have power to supply, from the local rates, the school-pence of poor parents, though they were not in receipt of out-door relief. A measure for establishing a rate in aid of school incomes cannot

---

part of the school. This is so obviously probable a result, that I should not have thought it important to ascertain the facts had not the opposite doctrine been asserted with so much pertinacity. These inquiries were, however, made before the purely artificial arrangement of the school according to the Standards of the Revised Code was introduced by teachers.

* See p. 76.

be successful in opposition to the feelings and opinions of the religious communions; and it would lack both stability and efficiency, if it did not obtain the active co-operation of the landed proprietors and of the intelligent and educated portions of the middle classes of rural parishes. A District Education Committee and a Local Committee, both elected by the rate-payers, would think more of economy in the administration of the school fund than of the efficiency of the schools, and would soon be in direct conflict with the clergy and gentry. Every precaution therefore should be adopted, to place the district administration in the hands of the most intelligent and influential persons, and to ensure that the parochial school Committee should be composed of elements which would work in harmony with the regulations of the Committee of Privy Council.

Considering, also, how very recent is the growth of anything like a local, civil, or political interest in education, it may be well to co-ordinate the authority of the Privy Council with that of the locality in the initiatory steps necessary for the introduction into any district of the power to raise rates towards the expense of founding and supporting schools. This mingling of the central and provincial power might be brought about by such preliminary inquiries and reports as those suggested by Mr. Lowe in his speech at Edinburgh. The Privy Council would not proceed without the certainty of sufficient local co-operation.

The consent of the tenant-farmers and tradesmen to the introduction of the school-rate in any district will be more readily obtained in proportion as they have any prospect of deriving benefit from the schools for the education of their children. These classes send their children to the schools aided and inspected by the Privy Council Committee when they are within their reach, and often in preference to the endowed grammar schools, because they prefer that their children should be thoroughly grounded in the common elements of a sound English education, rather than that they should obtain an imperfect knowledge of the classical languages. They would the more readily assent to the expenditure from the rates required to render the parochial school efficient—and to the regulations of the Education Department as to the qualifications and number of the teachers, and the subjects to be taught—if they could thus be more certain of obtaining a thoroughly useful education for their children. These, again, are among the reasons why the Education Department should not relax its requirements as to the certificate. They bring to mind the regulations reported by Mr. Matthew Arnold to be enforced by the Prussian law, that where a *superior* elementary school does not exist in any commune, the teacher of the *common* elementary school shall hold a higher certificate.

The maintenance of the standard of elementary education is the chief duty of the Education Department. The recent legislation making education a condition of employment, defines the period to which such instruction can be extended in the day school. The Education Department has to determine what are the qualifications and numbers of the teachers required to secure the largest amount of instruction attainable within this period. If the standard of education which can thus be given is below the political and industrial wants of the country, the instruction of youth may be continued in the evening school. Many of our principal manufacturers have, from the reported results of the Universal Exhibition at Paris, arrived at a conviction that a superior elementary education is necessary to enable our artisans to proceed to acquire such a knowledge of the scientific relations of the arts in which they are employed as may enable them to continue a successful competition with foreign rivals. The organization of the evening school is therefore a matter scarcely inferior in importance to that of the day school.

The evening school has, however, hitherto received little encouragement from the Education Department. The old code wisely forbade the Teacher to give instruction in an evening school, in order that his attention might be concentrated on the day school and on the instruction of his apprentices. This regulation arose from the conviction that five or six hours' teaching in the day school, and one hour and a half devoted to the instruction of the pupil teachers, together with the preparation of lessons for the following day's work, were an exhaustive labour.

No aid was, however, given to evening schools until 1855, when a grant was made to encourage the employment of local teachers in them when connected with inspected day schools, and taught by certificated teachers. Three years later (July 26th, 1858) the Capitation Grant of 1853 was extended to evening schools, in order "to provide the means of engaging a " second certificated teacher, who may assist in the morning " school, singly take the afternoon school, and, if not employed " in the special instruction of the pupil teachers, assist in the " night school which the principal teacher himself will be able " to conduct."

By the Revised Code all these regulations are changed. The teacher of the day school is not prevented from also conducting the evening school. He may instruct his pupil teachers in this school. He is thus relieved of the labour of teaching them separately during one hour and a half daily. But he is not provided with any help in the management of the evening school, and the pupil teachers have to take their chance of getting what instruction they can when the teacher is overtasked with night work in a school of rough youth. There is, however, the inducement of a Capitation Grant of five shillings "for every " scholar who has attended more than twenty-four evening " meetings of their school, subject to examination."* This examination may be conducted by the Managers, who are for that purpose furnished with printed papers and instructions, after forty or more meetings of the school have occurred since the last visit† of the Inspector.

It is important first to ascertain what inducements these articles of the Revised Code give teachers to found evening schools. That Code has reduced their salaries. The average salaries of masters were in 1862–3‡ reported to be 94*l.* 18*s.* 7*d.*, and in 1866–7, 87*l.* 3*s.*; while those of mistresses were (1862–3) 62*l.* 13*s.* 7*d.* and (1866–7) 55*l.* 0*s.* 2*d.* The Committee of Council report in 1865–6§ that " in some cases the managers " exhibit an inclination to throw the whole pecuniary risk on " the teachers—thereby reducing the schools to the level of " private adventure." I have already said that there are districts in which this arrangement is common. The obvious result is to create a strong motive for the establishment of an evening school by the teacher, in order that he may increase his income. But in a former part of this memorandum it is shown that the teaching staff of the day school has been so far reduced, that, whereas in 1861 there was one pupil teacher for every 36 scholars, in 1866–7 there was only one pupil teacher for every 54 scholars. The teaching power in the day school is further impaired by the comparative neglect of the instruction of the pupil teachers, who become less efficient assistants, and by the exhaustion of the energy of the principal teacher in the evening school. Under such circumstances, the night school can succeed only in proportion as the principal teacher reserves his strength for it, at the expense of the day school, and of the instruction of his pupil teachers. The degree in which evening schools are founded in any district, and the number of their scholars, may now be regarded as a pretty accurate measure of the deterioration of the day schools.

It has been with much pain that I have witnessed the growth of this system in a district with which I am familiar. Before the adoption of the Revised Code, there were in East Lancashire few evening schools which were not connected with Mechanics' Institutions, or which were not purely supplementary to Sunday Schools, and then taught solely by voluntary

---

* Revised Code, Article 40, clause (*c.*), p. xliv., Minutes, 1866–7.
† Ibid., p. lxxxvii., Articles 142–*142 to 149.
‡ Minutes, 1862–3 (p. 4), and 1866–7 (p. 5).   § Ibid., p. xvi.

teachers. There was also an average attendance of nearly 1,800 young persons and adults in the evening classes of the Mechanics' Institutions. In 1867 there were in East Lancashire (forty-six for males and thirty-two for females) seventy-eight evening schools, most of them connected with inspected day schools, taught by certificated teachers.

These evening schools were conducted by sixty certificated and nineteen other paid teachers, besides voluntary assistants. The scholars on the registers amounted to 4,867, and the average attendance was 3,289, or there was one paid teacher for every 41·63 scholars. The evening classes of the Mechanics' Institutions had still 1,219 scholars on their registers, and an average attendance of 842.

Such a system of evening schools is illusory. Whatever success it obtains is at the expense of the day schools, and in spite of the insufficient preparation of the scholars who leave the day schools to enter the evening schools. The day school suffers, because the teacher is exhausted in the night school; which in its turn suffers, both because it is conducted by an over-taxed teacher, and because it receives ill-educated scholars. *Neither of these classes of schools can succeed without an adequate staff of trained teachers, whose energies are not worn out by excessive work.*

Apparently, the public are in earnest in the expression of their desire that the day and evening schools shall be so efficient as to lay the basis of popular instruction firmly. They thus hope that some of our youth may be prepared to receive instruction in superior schools, and that a selected portion of them may acquire such knowledge as may promote the success of our industry by the influence of science and art. If the desire so loudly expressed arise from a deliberate and settled conviction that such higher education is necessary to the continuance of the success of our competition with foreign rivals, then the Committee of Council on Education will have to adopt such regulations as will secure a thoroughly efficient staff of well-trained teachers, both in day and in evening schools. The influence of the Revised Code has been to diminish both the number and the skill of this staff, and to wear out their strength in almost fruitless labour.

In the evening schools of Mechanics' Institutions, the plan of grouping schools for greater economy in the introduction of a trained teaching staff has been successfully in operation for ten years in the East Lancashire Union of Institutions. The idea of this organization included the following arrangements in each evening school. A Candidate Teacher to correspond with the Pupil Teacher of the day school. A paid Local Teacher to correspond with the Assistant Teacher of the day school when selected from the Pupil Teachers at the close of their apprenticeship. An itinerant Certificated Teacher who visited, organized, and taught three separate evening schools, each on two evenings in every week, and superintended the studies of the Candidate and Local Teachers. This Itinerant (called the Organizing) Master also held certificates from the Science and Art Department, and conducted science classes. The Committee of Council on Education during one year aided this scheme by grants in aid of the salaries of the Local Teachers, and by allowing the Organizing Master to obtain the augmentation then given to all Certificated Masters. Then, during the winter of economy which preceded and followed the Revised Code, this aid was withdrawn. Now the evening schools of the Mechanics' Institutions have, without any aid from the Government, to compete with the evening schools founded by the teachers of day schools, and aided by the Capitation Grant, to the great injury of the day schools. These are certainly not skilful combinations, if the intention of the Education Department be to promote the efficiency of primary instruction, and to encourage the spontaneous efforts of the manual-labour class for self-improvement. It is difficult to conceive how any one with a knowledge of the facts can have permitted such combinations to exist, or when their mischievous tendency was proved, can have permitted them to continue. A system which depends on spontaneous zeal for the initiation, if it be without sympathy and without generosity, is suicidal. A mere red-tape administration of the Parliamentary Grant by rigid rules, with the intention, before all things, of preventing the growth of the charge, meets all the new claims of spontaneous zeal with insurmountable technical difficulties, and is soon the antagonist of the initiatory power. It is possible to combine a statesmanlike providence of the national fund with a wise and farsighted policy in the encouragement of all true and earnest voluntary efforts.

The same plan of grouping might be applied to the evening schools connected with day schools, and without any other objection than that arising from expense, provided no part of the teaching staff of the day school were employed. But all such expedients as the employment of the Certificated Night School Teacher to conduct the day school during half the day, and so release the principal teacher during that half of the day, in order that he may teach in the evening, are not found to work well. The Certificated Teacher who has not a personal responsibility for the day school does not, however able, adequately supply the place of the responsible teacher. A conscientious teacher refuses to do more under such circumstances than accept the aid of the Certificated Night School Teacher, but continues also to labour without intermission in his day school, and also takes his part in the night school. The intention of the arrangement, which is to prevent the exhaustion of the principal Day School Teacher, is thus frustrated. I give in a note an estimate of the cost of such an organization of evening schools independently of day schools.*

Mr. Mundella and Mr. Samuelson † both claim, at least for the youth who are to be trained to become the overlookers of skilled labour, first, that our day schools shall turn out their scholar *well prepared for superior instruction.* Secondly, that the most promising pupils shall be *enabled to avail themselves of whatever means exist for higher education* by such encouragement as has been provided by a recent minute of the Science and Art Department. It is obvious that the night school ought to be regarded as an indispensable link in this chain, especially in consideration that labour is allowed to claim one half of the time of children until they are thirteen years of age, and often their whole time after they are twelve years old.

As my chief object in this Memorandum is an analysis of that which exists, and has been subjected to the test of experience, or has undergone discussion in Parliament, I make no comments here on the recent minute of the Science and Art Department, except that, as that Department is, equally with

---

* The cost of a group of these night schools, organized independently of day schools, may be estimated as follows, if the use of the school books, apparatus, school-rooms, fuel, and cleaning be granted by the committee of the day school without charge:—

	£	s.	d.
Average stipends of three Local Teachers, graduated at an increasing annual rate, 15*l.* each	45	0	0
Average graduated stipends of three Candidate Teachers	30	0	0
Salary of one Certificated Teacher, with liberty to conduct science classes, or to employ one half the day as a school assistant	75	0	0
	£150	0	0

If sixty scholars attended each school, there would be one teacher for every twenty scholars, and the average cost per head would be 16*s.* 8*d.* At present the payments of the night scholars do not exceed 2*d.* per week, or 2*s.* per quarter, but schools are often open during nine months. In such cases, 6*s.* might now be derived from school-pence. If 7*s.* 6*d.* were available from the Parliamentary Grant, much progress would soon be made. If one Local Teacher and one Candidate Teacher only be employed on every night in the week in the three schools, their services might be engaged for 24*l.* and 12*l.* respectively, or at most for 30*l.* and 15*l.* Thus 30*l.* would be saved, and the cost reduced to 13*s.* 4*d.* per night scholar.

† See copy of letter from B. Samuelson, Esq., M.P., to the Vice-President of the Committee of Council on Education, concerning 'Technical Education in various Countries Abroad,' p. 57.

the Education Department, under the direction of the Committee of Council on Education, they ought to work in harmony. And further, to proceed simply on the guarantee of inspection, and the idea that the *minimum of results* can determine what schools ought to be entrusted with the training of youth for higher instruction, is, if the analysis of this Memorandum has brought out correct issues, a fallacy which should cease to have any form of public sanction.

Nor do I think it convenient here to point out the natural way in which day schools, for the higher instruction of youth taught until thirteen years old in the elementary schools, are arising out of the impulse to education given by the Minutes of 1846, and the first Code embodying them.

Owen's College, at Manchester, under the guidance of able professors, and an enlightened body of Trustees, is exploring the path towards the foundation and support of provincial Schools for technical instruction, according to the wants of the several centres of our manufactures and commerce. As respects Mining, the Government have founded a Model School in Jermyn-street, capable of being developed into a *College teaching what are the practical relations of science and art to our industry and commerce.* But all these separate efforts require to be co-ordinated by some presiding intelligence. For this reason, and because of the work which has to be done in the Reform of Charitable Endowments* of Education—in the public and private schools of the Middle Classes—and in the great foundation schools of the wealthiest and most aristocratic, the time is arrived when the proposal pressed in the Report submitted by Sir John Pakington to the Parliamentary Committee over which he presided should be adopted, *viz.* that the Department of Education and Charitable Endowments should be presided over by a Minister of State, who should be a member of the Cabinet.

The extension of the electoral power to the mass of the people must be followed by grave consequences, as well in the action of the legislative as of the executive authority. It is not within the functions of a constituency to settle the details of legislation. To refer such matters to it would be to give it credit for knowledge, foresight, and judicial calmness, which are the rare attributes only of the few men, whose genius, after years of training, enables them to guide Parliament, and to give sagacious counsels in the Cabinet. But the instinctive impulses of the popular electoral body will be strong ; sometimes they may

---

* See paper on "Charitable Endowments for Education" in volume of Transactions of Social Science Association,' 1866-7.

even be uncontrollable. *They will discern an end which they wish to attain.* They will select the men in whom they most confide as their surest and ablest instruments to attain this end. To their experience, wisdom, earnestness, and patriotism—according to their estimate of these qualities—they will entrust the accomplishment of this work. They will invigorate them with their confidence, and invest them with all the power which can be derived from popular support. They will demand that the strength thus given shall be used promptly, vigorously, effectually. All this tends, as all real democratic government has ultimately tended, to *strengthen the Executive.* Parliament, as a deliberative body, will have to give form and expression to the instinctive will of the constituency, but the Executive will have a double duty: *First,* to supply Parliament with all necessary information, and to place before it projects of law for discussion, as well as to aid and guide its deliberations : *Secondly,* to carry firmly and faithfully the decisions of Parliament into execution, as the articulate expressions of the national will.

The instinctive cry of this will is now to be the voice, not of the middle classes, as it has been since 1832, but of the entire mass of the people, including the wealthiest and most privileged, but also—as never before—the humblest classes. If there be an earnest, eager, persevering cry for anything within the limits of Parliamentary power, that object of desire will have to be conceded. But to statesmen is reserved the function of giving that form to the execution of the instinctive national desire which shall be most consistent with the traditions and the permanent interests of the country.

To apply these anticipations to the subject of national education. If there be a deep-seated, earnest conviction in the new electoral body, that the education of the mass of the people can be no longer safely deferred, every obstacle to the accomplishment of this enterprise will be swept away, like barriers of sand before the tide, and every institution which resists will be like a vessel, the sport of a raging and overwhelming surf.

It may be well before concluding to summarize some of the chief results of this analysis.

1. The system of promoting the extension and improvement of elementary education by the Schools of the religious Communions has provided better means for the instruction of one million and a quarter of children than any which have yet been brought into operation.

2. The grants of the Committee of Council on Education have created a system for the training of teachers, and for

supplying a teaching staff to schools, deficient only in the imperfection of the conditions of assistance, and in a distinct and clear perception of the fact, that the chief function of that Committee tends to be the maintenance of the efficiency of the instruction by means of a highly instructed and complete teaching machinery, and that this function cannot be, without mischief, delegated by the central to any local authority.

3. This combined system of State grants, in aid of the contributions and exertions of local voluntary agencies, is too deeply rooted in the social organization, traditions, and sentiments of the country to yield either to any temporary storm of opinion, or to the shock of administrative innovation. It is stronger than anything which could be substituted for it, and may calmly defy all adverse forces.

4. But this combined system is weak in the power of the initiative, and in order to supply the wants of the country, if education is to be made universal, it may be expedient to give to the Privy Council and to the provincial district a regulated and limited authority to take initiatory steps.

5. As the consequence and form of the expression of this initiatory power, facilities to raise a school-rate, in aid of the existing resources of schools, may have to be granted, but these must be so ordered as not to disturb the connection of schools with the religious Communions, nor the authority of the present Committees of Management, nor the religious constitution of the schools, but also so as to render their income less precarious, their efficiency greater, and the means of providing them more abundant.

6. By the force of this new power we might hope to extend the benefits of aid and inspection to all the now unaided schools, and to found similar schools in all neglected or apathetic districts.

7. There would then co-exist: (a) The Committee of Council on Education providing one-third of the income of schools from the Parliamentary Grant, and regulating by its Code of Minutes and Inspection the standard and objects of National Education and the training of teachers.   (b) The Committees of Managers superintending and directing all the details of school discipline, organization, and instruction, and providing from school-pence and voluntary agencies a second third of the income.   (c) The remaining third would be furnished by the District Education Committee, who would derive it from a school-rate, and who, besides being primarily responsible for making provision for neglected districts, and for the education of the children of indigent parents, would also have local charge of the impartial distribution of the school-rate fund on recognized public prin-

ciples, and of the representation of the interests of the rate-
payers, and of the parents of scholars.

8. The principle of securing for children under thirteen or
fourteen years of age a sufficient time for education should be
extended to farming occupations, and to the children—not at
work—of parents receiving out-door relief. But no other mode
of compulsory education should at present be adopted.

9. The Code of Minutes of the Committee of Council would
continue to regulate the distribution of the Parliamentary Grant,
but it would be necessary to modify this so as to secure the following objects:—

(a) That the Inspectors should have time, as well for the
general inspection of the school, and for an examination of the
higher subjects of instruction, as for the individual examination
of the scholars in the elements.

(b) By the graduation of the Capitation Grants, to give to
the Managers adequate motives to appoint a sufficient number of
Pupil Teachers, and to the principal teachers an interest in
their successful education. To afford a reward for the successful
cultivation of the higher as well as the lower subjects of instruction. To reduce to the minimum the fundamental objections to
a Capitation Grant, by making the amount which depends on
individual examination smaller.

(c) To adopt every method to encourage and make stable
the apprenticeship of Pupil Teachers—as distinguished from their
hiring—and thus to provide a sufficient supply of well-educated
Candidates for the Training Colleges, and of efficient teachers
for the extension of the present school system.

(d) To promote the spread of sound education in the
neglected districts and small parishes, by making Provisional
Grants to schools for two years, dependent on the results of examination, and on the fulfilment of the usual terms of aid at the
end of two years.

(e) To encourage by the Minutes, as a primary intention,
the founding and support only of thoroughly good and efficient
schools, and to regard every inferior result as a waste of public
resources.

JAMES P. KAY-SHUTTLEWORTH.

38, *Gloucester Square, Hyde Park, W.*
January 24th, 1868.

TABLE No. I.—Aggregate Local Income (as returned by the Managers) of an ascertained number of Schools, extracted from Minutes of Committee of Council on Education in each year.

YEAR	Number of Schools making these Returns	Average Income for Scholars in Attendance	From Endowment	From Voluntary Contributions	INCOME. From Other Sources	Total without School-pence	From School-pence	Total with School-pence	Number of Children on the Average in Attendance in these Schools
		s. d.	*£ s. d.*	*£ s. d.*	*£ s. d.*	*£ s. d.*	*£ s. d.*	*£ s. d.*	
1860	5980	17 3½	50,287 9 6	270,187 9 2	72,182 8 1	392,657 6 9	302,731 2 9	695,388 9 6	803,708
1861	6457.	17 5½	50,890 19 3	281,531 18 10	87,593 15 2	420,016 13 3	326,110 5 4	746,126 18 7	855,077
1862	6568	17 5¾	51,377 15 3	287,441 5 8	103,618 8 10	442,437 9 8	334,819 2 4	777,256 12 0	888,923
1863	6851	17 3¼	51,865 1 6	291,189 11 8	101,985 7 6	445,040 0 8	356,739 17 8	801,779 18 4	928,310
1864	7064	18 0¾	47,767 7 1	314,993 5 0	105,423 4 8	468,183 16 9	378,888 16 6	847,072 13 3	937,678
1865	7610	18 2½	55,285 19 9	352,748 10 9	97,281 3 6	505,315 14 0	420,947 10 4	926,263 4 4	1,016,558
1866	8049	18 6½	55,364 14 10	366,182 3 8	103,962 2 1	525,509 0 7	446,737 4 10	972,246 5 5	1,048,493

TABLE No. II. Showing Number of Certificated Teachers actually employed in Teaching; Number of Assistant Teachers appointed under Minute of July, 1852; Number of Probationary Teachers appointed under Minute of July, 1858; and Number of Pupil Teachers under Apprenticeship.—(Corrected to 31st December, 1860.)

| | Certificated Teachers | | | Assistant Teachers | | | Probationary Teachers | | | Pupil Teachers | | | | | | | | | | | | | | | | | Total | | |
| | | | | | | | | | | 1st Year | | | 2nd Year | | | 3rd Year | | | 4th Year | | | 5th Year | | | | | |
	Male	Female	Total	Male	Female	Total	Male	Female	Total	Male	Female	Total	Male	Female	Total	Male	Female	Total	Male	Female	Total	Male	Female	Total	Male	Female	Total
England ..	3283	2758	6041	158	75	233	168	79	247	1072	1123	2195	1420	1380	2800	1353	1438	2791	1283	1296	2579	1031	987	2018	6159	6224	12,383
Wales	268	84	352	10	6	16	32	..	32	82	26	108	120	59	179	117	55	172	100	60	160	95	44	139	514	244	758
Isle of Man and Channel Islands	26	14	40	1	..	1	..	1	1	11	7	18	10	6	16	14	12	26	11	7	18	6	12	18	52	44	96
Scotland ..	943	335	1278	43	2	45	38	5	43	299	126	425	358	141	499	340	180	520	290	132	422	311	121	432	1598	700	2,298
Total	4520	3191	7711	212	83	295	238	85	323	1464	1282	2746	1908	1586	3494	1824	1685	3509	1684	1495	3179	1443	1164	2607	8323	7212	15,535

TABLE No. III.—Number of Certificated Assistant Teachers, Probationary and Pupil Teachers.

YEAR ENDING.	Certificated Teachers.	Assistant Teachers.	Probationary Teachers.	Pupil Teachers.	Average Attendance of Scholars.
December 31st, 1860	7,711	295	323	15,535	919,935
December 31st, 1861	8,698	381	491	16,277	
December 31st, 1862	9,115	449	518	15,752	
December 31st, 1863	10,136	461	..	14,180	
December 31st, 1864	10,809	688	..	12,161	
December 31st, 1865	11,510	912	..	11,221	1,057,745*
December 31st, 1866	12,179	1061	..	10,971	1,082,055*

Pupil Teachers.   Assistant Teachers.   Probationary Teachers.

In 1861 there were.. .. .. .. : 16,277 .. 381 .. 491
872 Assistant and Probationary Teachers,} = 1,744
each reckoned as two Pupil Teachers }

8698 Certificated Teachers .. .. : 18,021 with 919,935 scholars on the average in attendance, or equal to 36 for each pupil teacher, if the assistants and probationary teachers are each reckoned as two pupil teachers, and if 30 scholars are assigned to the principal teacher.

In 1866 there were 10,971 pupil teachers and 1061 assistant teachers.
2,122

13,093 with 1,082,055 scholars in average attendance, or if 30 scholars be assigned to each principal teacher, and each assistant be reckoned as two pupil teachers, then each pupil teacher would have 54 scholars.

* See Minutes, 1866–67, p. ix.   Returns to August 31.

TABLE No. IV.—Returns of the Number of Candidates presented for Examination at Training Colleges; the Number who passed their Examinations; the Number who entered Training Colleges; the Number of Pupil Teachers Apprenticed; and the Number of Pupil Teachers in each of the years of Apprenticeship, 1861–6.

	1861.			1862.			1863.			1864.			1865.			1866.		
	Males.	Females.	Total.	Males.	Females.	Total.	Males.	Females.	Total.	Males.	Females.	Total.	Males.	Females.	Total.	Males.	Females.	Total.
Number of Candidates who presented themselves for Examination at the Training Colleges	1174	1299	2473	1128	1385	2513	789	1042	1831	591	904	1495	608	947	1555	616	968	1584
Number who passed the Examination	869	858	1727	990	993	1983	691	791	1482	518	810	1328	521	785	1306	450	756	1207
Number who entered Training Colleges	..	..	..	821	770	1591	913	842	1755	594	694	1288	501	697	1198	508	707	1215
Number of Pupil Teachers admitted to Apprenticeship	..	..	2984	..	..	2762	..	..	2971	1228	1340	2568	1338	1293	2631	1450	1620	3070
Number of Pupil Teachers:																		
1st year	1521	1571	3092	1454	1480	2934	1160	1155	2315	884*	1011*	1895	1212*	1143*	2355	1311*	1409*	2720
2nd year	1653	1586	3239	1598	1672	3270	1431	1521	2952	1077	1198	2275	885	1063	1948	1169	1324	2493
3rd year	1799	1558	3357	1522	1484	3006	1521	1619	3140	1281	1383	2664	929	1152	2081	792	1000	1792
4th year	1768	1704	3472	1712	1526	3238	1375	1411	2786	1242	1489	2731	1106	1272	2378	799	1073	1872
5th year	1654	1463	3117	1682	1627	3309	1556	1431	2987	1241	1355	2596	1075	1384	2459	961	1133	2094‡

* These numbers are less than those immediately above them; but Pupil Teachers, who are old and proficient enough, are often "admitted" in one of the later years of service.

TABLE No. V.—Number of Candidates for Admission to Training Colleges; the Number who passed the Entrance Examination; the Number of Resident Students who passed each year's Examination; the Number Resident and Leaving each year; and the Number of Admissions.

Examination at Christmas.	Candidates for Admission.			Passed the Examination.	Students in Training Colleges who have passed Examinations.		Number of Students Resident in Year preceding.	Number who Left at the preceding Christmas.	Number of Admissions at Christmas of the Year named.	Number Resident in March of the Year named.
	Pupil Teachers.	Non-Pupil Teachers.	Total.		First Year.	Second Year.				
1860	..	..	..	2604	..	2655	..	..	..	2616
1861	..	..	..	..	..	..	2869	1663	1841	3047
1862	..	..	..	..	..	..	2972*	1641	1921	3252†
1863	..	..	1831	1482	1721	1239	3109	1655	1285	2739
1864	1286	209	1495	1328	1287	1279	2633	1426	1275	2482
1865	1324	231	1555	1306	1191	1113	2482	1358	1283	2407
1866	1318	266	1584	1207	1218	1024	2403	1256	1213	2360

* December, 1862.   † March, 1863.

TABLE No. VI.—Income and Expenditure of Training Colleges in Great Britain.

December 31st.	Income from Government.			Income from Local Sources.			Total Income.			Expenditure.		
	£	s.	d.	£	s.	d.	£	s.	d.	£	s.	d.
1861	101,156	7	11	23,623	11	7	124,779		6	98,130	5	6
1862	103,585	14	2	25,264			128,849	14	2	126,238	6	11
1863	113,241	17	1	19,871	5	7	133,113	2	8	106,759	9	4
1864	96,166	16	10	25,074	7	5	121,241	4	3	121,385	5	1
1865	74,013	1	9	27,494	1	9	101,507			101,614	11	5
1866	74,873	2	3	27,820	1	9	102,693	4	0	100,866	6	10
1866 compared with 1861	− 26,283	5	8	+ 4,196	10	2	− 22,086		6	+ 2,736	1	4
1866 compared with 1862	− 28,712	11	11	+ 2,556	1	9	− 26,156	16	11	− 25,372	0	1

The plus and minus results when each head of Income and Expenditure in 1861 and 1862 is compared with the same head in 1866.

APPENDIX No. VII.

Extract from Report of Committee of Council on Education for 1866-7, pp. xii., xiii., xiv.

Mistresses are cheaper to employ than masters. In schools generally, salaries bear the ratio of 75 per cent. to the total expenditure; and, inasmuch as the salaries of competent teachers cannot descend below a certain minimum, whether few children have to be taught by them or many, this minimum bears an increased ratio to the rest of the expenditure in very small schools. The minimum salary of a certificated mistress may be set down as a guaranteed receipt of 40*l.* per annum, with a furnished house or lodgings. Mr. Tinling, in his Report of last year (pp. 430-6), gives the salaries obtained by female students on leaving 13 out of the 14 colleges inspected by him, and in five colleges he sets it down as 40*l.* with a furnished house. The experienced mistresses of important schools obtain higher rates, which raise the average (infra, p. 5), but mistresses quite competent to manage, with the help of a female pupil teacher, schools of 60 or 70 children where the boys do not stay much beyond their tenth year completed, may be engaged towards the end of each year, for commencement of service in the next, at the rate of 40*l.* per annum and furnished lodgings, from the training colleges (infra, p. 369). The cost per annum therefore of such a school will not be less than:—

Mistress's Salary	£40
Female Pupil Teacher's (average)	10
Other Expenses..	17
	£67

If the scholars do not exceed 64, there is nothing in our Code, nor in our recent Minute, which requires a pupil teacher to be maintained. Up to this limit, managers are at liberty to supplement the teacher's efforts with their own, or with any other unpaid assistance they can command. Assuming then a school attended on the average by 64 children, including the ordinary proportion of infants, the cost per annum might be reduced to 57*l.*, and the grants might very well be as follows: or if so much was not actually paid, the reason would be that the amount must not (under Article 52, c. 1) exceed half the expenditure:—

	£	s.	d.
Grants of 4*s.* each on 64, average number attending school (Article 40*a*)	12	16	0
Grants of 4*s.* per pass on 103 passes, being the average number now obtained by schools of this size (Article 40, b. 1, and Minute 20 February, 1867)	20	12	0
24 infants at 6*s.* 6*d.* each (Article 40, b. 2)	7	16	0
	£41	4	0

The half, however, of 57*l.* is only 28*l.* 10*s.*, and therefore while the grant is not to exceed this latter amount, the above calculation shows how little likely it is to fall below it. The fees paid by 64 scholars ought to average not less than 2*d.* per week for 40 weeks in the year; and they yield, on this estimate, 21*l.* 6*s.* 8*d.*, leaving only 7*l.* 3*s.* 4*d.* to be raised by subscription. If, in deference to the custom which remains in some parishes of charging only 1*d.* per week, the fees be reduced to one-half, or 10*l.* 13*s.* 4*d.*, the sum remaining to be subscribed is 17*l.* 16*s.* 8*d.* A school attended on the average by 64 children will have about 85 on its books (Report of Royal Commission, 1861, p. 573), and will suffice for a population of about 500 or rather more. If the number of children is assumed to be 40 instead of 64, the item of "salary" will remain the same, and little more of "other expenses" will be reduced than represents books—say 2*l.* in the whole. Towards raising then the sum of 55*l*. wanted to educate 40 children, the grant may be estimated to yield:—

				£	*s.*	*d.*
4*s*. per child attending	..	..	..	.. 8	0	0
4*s*. on 64 passes	..	..	..	.. 12	16	0
6*s*. 6*d*. on 16 infants	..	..	..	.. 5	4	0
				£26	0	0

The fees (as above) will yield either 6*l*. 13*s*. 4*d*., or 13*l*. 6*s*. 8*d*., and the subscriptions will have to be either 15*l*. 13*s*. 4*d*. or 22*l*. 6*s*. 8*d*. to make up the total of 55*l*.

Appendix No. VIII.

Memorandum communicated by Alexander Redgrave, Esq., *one of Her Majesty's Inspectors of Factories, as to the Progress of Legislation for the Protection of the Labour of Women, Young Persons, and Children; and as to the Education of Children.*

The first Factory Act (42 Geo. III. c. 73, 1802) was an attempt to remedy the evils of excessive labour in Cotton and Woollen Factories only; and for years afterwards the manufacture of textile fabrics only was placed under Legislative restrictions. Thus the Factory Acts of 1833 and 1844, with their amending Acts, dealt only with labour in the actual spinning and manufacture of textile fabrics, as they existed at the time, *viz.*: of Cotton, Wool, Worsted. Hemp, Flax, Tow, Silk, or Jute. The next series of Acts had still reference only to textile fabrics, *viz.*: Printworks, and the Bleaching, Dyeing, and finishing of textile goods. Various modifications of the Factory Regulations were conceded to these works, on the ground of their inapplicability to the peculiarities and necessities of the trades. An inquiry is now being made into the validity of the grounds upon which these modifications were permitted, with a view to remedy many defects which have been greatly complained of. Another Act, the first fruits of the Children's Employment Commission, was passed in 1864. This extended the Factory Regulations to a variety of trades, *viz.*: to the manufacture of earthenware, of lucifer matches, of percussion caps and cartridges, to the employments of paper-staining and of fustian-cutting. In all these trades the greatest satisfaction has been expressed by the masters at the results of the application to their premises of Factory Regulations. They co-operate with the Inspectors, and have experienced none of the inconveniences and difficulties which they had anticipated, while the operatives are no less satisfied at the beneficial operation of the new system.

Following very closely the outline of the Act of 1864, the Legislature endeavoured in the Session of 1867 to cope with every kind of labour, exercised in the way of trade, for the production of an article for sale.

First, the "Factory Acts Extension Act, 1867," which places under the regulations of the Factory Acts the following premises, *viz.*:—

Blast furnaces, copper mills, iron mills and forges, foundries; premises whereon steam or water power is used to manufacture machinery, or any article of metal, or of India-rubber or gutta-percha; premises in which are carried on paper, glass, or tobacco manufactures; letter-press printing or bookbinding. In addition to the preceding, any other premises on which at least fifty persons are employed on any manual labour, for any process in the preparing or finishing of any article for sale.

The Government, in the first instance, and afterwards the Committee of the House of Commons, considered with great attention the representations made from the different trades proposed to be brought under restrictions, of the inconveniences and injuries which would be caused to many trades, by a strict and close adherence to the Factory Regulations as in force in cotton and other factories, and various *temporary* modifications were granted for the purpose of making the transition from unlimited to limited labour more gradual. Other *permanent* modifications were also agreed to, in order to provide against very serious interruptions to processes of manufacture, and disturbance of existing customs and habits, which were threatened by the strict Factory Law.

But the following regulations are absolute :—

1. The prohibition of the night-work of women and children.

2. The limitation of the night-work of young persons in some specified trades, such as blast-furnaces, paper-mills, &c., to not more than six nights in a fortnight, and the prohibition of day-work during the night turn.

3. The limitation of the hours of work of children to half the day, *with the obligation of daily school attendance.*

4. The limitation of the hours of work of young persons and women to 10.30 hours per day, and 60 hours per week.

5. The other ordinary rules as to meals and holidays, dangerous machinery and accidents.

6. The original Factory Acts made no provision for securing proper ventilation and cleanliness, but by the two last Acts, 1864 and 1867, these two important conditions must be observed; and by the last Act, 1867, the further obligation is enacted, that means shall be provided for preventing the inhalation by workmen of dust, gas, or other impurities caused by any process of manufacture.

The preceding Acts embrace all the large and important classes of Factories. Their administration has been placed under the supervision of the Inspectors of Factories, and the machinery of the Factory Acts applies to them all. The details as to Surgical Certificates as proof of age — the registration of names, &c., in Factories of the smallest class would be irksome and to a great extent unnecessary. The Legislature therefore proceeded to lay down rules to be observed in all these minor classes of labour, which are not included in any of the above Factory Acts, without the minute details to which the larger Works are subjected, and passed the "Workshops Regulation Act, 1867."

This Act applies to all manual labour exercised by way of Trade in preparing or finishing any article for sale.

The main features of the "Factory Acts Extension Act, 1867," are adopted, except that the labour of Young Persons and Women may be extended to 12 hours per day, between wider limits than under the Factory Acts : *i. e.*, they may commence at 5 a.m. and need not cease until 9 p.m. ; and on Saturdays work may be continued after the regular hours in shops wherein more than five persons are employed in *repairing* articles; the school attendance of children need not exceed 10 hours per week instead of 15, as under the Factory Acts. Temporary and permanent modifications very similar to those in the "Factory Acts Extension Act, of 1867," are also included in the Workshops Act.

The administration of the Workshops Act is not placed in the hands of the Inspectors of Factories, but is enjoined upon the Local Authority, whether Mayor, Provost, Board of Health, Vestry, or whatever may be the Governing Body of the locality. It is of great importance that these various bodies should accept the "duty" imposed upon them by the Act, for in their hands now rests the power of creating a school-seeking race of children. *Every* child who performs any manual labour (except in agriculture) is bound now to attend school concurrently with its daily occupation, but the system cannot be inaugurated unless by the influence and pressure of some governing body. The Inspectors of Factories are empowered to enter Workshops and consequently to enforce the provisions of the Act, but the intention of the Act seems rather that they should ascertain whether the Regulations of the Act have been administered by the Local Authorities. There is one provision of the Workshops Act which may be of great importance. It is that relating to the disqualifying of Schoolmasters. Under the Factory Acts, an Inspector is empowered to disqualify a Schoolmaster "by reason of his incapacity "to teach the children to read and write, from his gross ignorance, or from his not "having the materials necessary to teach reading and writing, or because of his im- "moral conduct," &c. The cause for disqualification is here clearly enough defined, but it reaches only the very worst class of cases, about which there could be no kind of doubt in the mind of the Inspector. The Workshops Regulation Act enlarges very much the grounds of disqualification, and it should be observed that no authority is given in respect to Schools, and School Certificates, to the Local Authority, these subjects being placed entirely under the control of the Inspectors of Factories. After repeating as grounds for disqualification the not filling up of certificates and immoral conduct, the Schoolmaster may be disqualified, if in the opinion of the Inspectors " he is unfit to teach children by reason either of his " ignorance or neglect, or of his not having the necessary books and materials." Under these terms there would be ample ground to disqualify many Schoolmasters, who cannot be interfered with under the Factory Acts, but whose continuance as Schoolmasters is disastrous. This power of disqualification, however, must be exercised with great caution and discretion, and should be used in most cases as a hidden source of influence, rather than as a direct act of authority.

The above Acts form a Code of Legislation, unexampled in any country in the world. The young and the weaker sex are absolutely secured from excessive labour : Children must and do attend School—all are protected from injuries, and the unhealthiness of processes is lessened. These great objects are obtained by the good feeling evinced by the Masters; by their appreciation of the just objects of the Legislature ; and by their ready acceptance of the obligations placed upon them.

APPENDIX IX.
Educational Inquiry in Manchester.

THIS Inquiry was undertaken by the Education Bill Committee, with a view to clear up some of the matters raised by the discussion upon the last Report of the Education Aid Society. The locality comprises two Wards of the Municipal Borough of Manchester, containing 92,517 Inhabitants.

It is bounded by the River Irk, Miller Street, Swan Street, Great Ancoats Street, Holt Town, the Borough Boundary at Miles Platting, across Oldham Road, and back to the Irk River. The method adopted was to copy the rate-books upon sheets ready ruled for the different headings, so that each line of a sheet would represent one house.

The Canvassers (who were all Ex-Police Inspectors or Relieving Officers, familiar with statistical inquiries) were simply instructed to study the headings of the sheets, and to see that all the questions were answered.

When the inquiry was nearly finished, the sheets were examined, and where errors appeared in any sheet from the figures not agreeing, were handed back to the Canvassers for a second visit, to insure their correction ; so that the return from every house can be referred to, if necessary, at any time.

St. Michael's Ward

comprises a population of 42,007 persons. 3,911 are from three to six years of age, and 50 per cent. of them have never been to a day-school, 4,289 are from six to ten years, and 10·2 per cent. of them have never been to a day-school ; 3,837 are from ten to fourteen years of age, and of these 7 per cent. have never been to a day-school. So that there appears to be only a small proportion of the population of this ward who, according to their own showing, do not, at some time or other, make an effort to secure instruction :—The total of children between three and fourteen years of age is 12,037, and of these 48 per cent. profess to be now going to school, 12·3 per cent. are at work (about one-tenth of whom are half-timers), and 39·2 per cent. are neither at school nor at work.

Of the 9,347 who are now, or have been to school,

20·8 per cent. are from three to six years of age.
41·1   ,,   six to ten   ,,
38·1   ,,   ten to fourteen   ,,

Of this number 2,580 have attended less than one year at school.

2,409	,,	,,	two	,,
1,778	,,	,,	three	,,
1,288	,,	,,	four	,,
684	,,	,,	five	,,
370	,,	,,	six	,,
136	,,	,,	seven	,,
66	,,	,,	eight	,,
29	,,	,,	nine	,,
5	,,	,,	ten	,,
2	,,	,,	eleven	,,

27·51 per cent. of the whole have therefore averaged half-a-year only; 25·5 per cent. have averaged one and a half year, and 19 per cent. two and a half years; so that 72 per cent. of the whole have averaged 1·38 year each, whilst the average of the whole number is 2·2 years, which, seeing that 38 per cent. of them have left school, will probably represent about the term of instruction reached by two-thirds of the pupils.

Only 28 per cent. have averaged 4·38 years, and this term has been very unequally shared, for 2·5 per cent. have had upwards of seven years of instruction each.

The value of the instruction received is tested by the condition of the youths of fourteen years of age and upwards, of whom there are 6,773. Of these youths 76·5 can read, and 62 per cent. only can write; so that, according to the parents' account, only 7 per cent. completely escape day-school instruction, 23·5 per cent. fail even to learn to read, and 38 per cent. fail to acquire the power to write their own names.

Of the children at school in this ward 22 per cent. were, at the end of September, assisted by the Education Aid Society.

The result of the inquiry is, therefore, that 52 per cent. of the children of the school age are not now at school, that work only hinders 12·3 per cent., and that of those who go to school 38 per cent. do not attain the ability to write their names, and 23·5 per cent. do not even learn to read.

NEW CROSS WARD.

The population of this ward is 50,510. Of this number 3,944 are from three to six years of age, and 51·8 per cent. of them have never been to a day-school, 4,444 are from six to ten years of age, and 13·8 per cent. have not been to a day-school; and 4,214 are from ten to fourteen years of age, and 9·6 per cent. of these have not been to a day-school. So that in this, as in St. Michael's Ward, an effort is made at some time or other by 90 per cent. of the population to get instruction; but much of this effort is evidently spasmodic, and therefore fruitless. The total of children from three to fourteen years of age is 12,602, of whom 37·4 per cent. are returned as now at school, 17·6 per cent. at work (about a quarter of whom are half-timers), whilst 44·9 per cent. are neither at school nor at work.

Of 9,549 who are returned as being now, or having been at some former time, at school—

2623 have attended less than one years	286 have attended less than seven years
2123 " " two "	138 " " eight "
1795 " " three "	56 " " nine "
1238 " " four "	25 " " ten "
769 " " five "	16 " " eleven "
480 " " six "	

Of the whole number 27·4 per cent. have averaged half-a-year only, 22·2 per cent. have averaged one and a half year, and 18·7 per cent. two and a half years each; so that 68·3 per cent. of the pupils have averaged only 1·37 year each, whilst the average of the whole is 2·3 years; and as 62·6 of the pupils are not now at school, it is difficult to see how any considerable proportion can get more than two years of instruction.

Under these circumstances it is not wonderful that, out of 8,102 youths of fourteen years and upwards, only 74 per cent. have learned to read, and 56·5 per cent. only have learned to write. Of the children at school in this ward, on the 29th September last, 1,559, or 33 per cent., were assisted by the Education Aid Society.

GENERAL SUMMARY.

The population of the two wards reported upon is 92,517. There are 7,855 children from three to six years of age, of whom 51 per cent. have never been to a day-school; 8,733 are from six to ten years of age, and 12 per cent. of these have never been to a day-school; 8,051 are from ten to fourteen years, and 8·3 per cent. of these have never been to a day-school. Thus, out of the total of 24,639 children between three and fourteen years of age, 76·6 per cent. have been for some short period to school, and only 8·3 per cent. reach fourteen years without seeing the inside of a day-school; but 9,592, or 50 per cent. of the whole, have been at some time chargeable to the Education Aid Society, so that, in the absence of that association, the state of things would have appeared much worse. Owing in great measure to want of funds, and owing also in a considerable degree to the careless-ness of parents in not using orders when granted, only about 13 per cent. of the present pupils are due to the Education Aid Society.

Whilst the present number returned as at school is 1 in 8·8 of the population, if we subtract the children sent by the Education Aid Society, it would be 1 in 11·3 only.

The difficulties of the Education Aid Society are illustrated by returns obtained from one school. Thus—from 1st May, 1865, to the present time—622 orders have been issued for that school. Of these orders, notwithstanding the utmost vigilance of the master in looking up the children, 53, or 10 per cent., have never been used; and of the 569 which have been used, only 143 are now in use.

But the saddest fact is, that the result of all our educational efforts, with Sunday Schools, Night Schools, and Literary Institutes included, still leaves 24·8 per cent. of our youths unable to read, and 58·4 per cent. unable to write.

le Duc